HISPANIC AMERICAN BIOGRAPHY

HISPANIC AMERICAN BIOGRAPHY

Volume 2: L-Z

Rob Nagel and Sharon Rose, *Editors*

An imprint of Gale Research Inc.,
an International Thomson Publishing Company

NEW YORK • LONDON • BONN • BOSTON • DETROIT • MADRID
MELBOURNE • MEXICO CITY • PARIS • SINGAPORE • TOKYO
TORONTO • WASHINGTON • ALBANY NY • BELMONT CA • CINCINNATI OH

HISPANIC AMERICAN BIOGRAPHY

Rob Nagel and Sharon Rose, *Editors*

Staff

Sonia Benson, *U·X·L Associate Developmental Editor*
Carol DeKane Nagel, *U·X·L Developmental Editor*
Thomas L. Romig, *U·X·L Publisher*

Arlene Johnson, *Permissions Associate (Pictures)*
Margaret A. Chamberlain, *Permissions Supervisor (Pictures)*

Mary Kelley, *Production Associate*
Evi Seoud, *Assistant Production Manager*
Mary Beth Trimper, *Production Director*

Mary Krzewinski, *Cover and Page Designer*
Cynthia Baldwin, *Art Director*

This book is printed on acid-free paper that meets the minimum requirements of American National Standard for Information Sciences—Permanence Paper for Printed Library Materials, ANSI Z39.48-1984.

ISBN 0-8103-9828-1 (Set)
ISBN 0-8103-9824-9 (Volume 1)
ISBN 0-8103-9825-7 (Volume 2)

Printed in the United States of America

I(T)P™ U·X·L is an imprint of Gale Research Inc.,
an International Thomson Publishing Company.
ITP logo is a trademark under license.

CONTENTS

CONTENTS

READER'S GUIDE

Hispanic American Biography profiles more than 90 Hispanic Americans, both living and deceased, prominent in fields ranging from civil rights to athletics, politics to literature, entertainment to science, religion to the military. The volumes also include Spanish founders and early leaders of Hispanic America as well as central figures of contemporary Hispanic cultural movements in the United States and in Latin America. A black-and-white portrait accompanies each entry, and a list of sources for further reading or research is provided at the end of each entry. Cross-references to other profiles in these volumes are noted in bold letters within the text. The volumes are arranged alphabetically and conclude with an index listing all individuals by fields of endeavor.

Related reference sources:

Hispanic American Almanac explores the history and culture of Hispanic America, a community of people in the United States whose ancestors—or they themselves—came from Spain or from the Spanish-speaking countries of South and Central America, Mexico, Puerto Rico, or Cuba. The *Almanac* is organized into 14 subject chapters, including immigration, family and religion, jobs and education, literature, and sports. The volume contains more than 70 black-and-white photographs and maps, a glossary, and a cumulative subject index.

Hispanic American Chronology explores significant social, political, economic, cultural, and educational milestones in Hispanic American history. Arranged by year and then by month and day, the chronology spans from 1492 to modern times and contains more than 70 illustrations, extensive cross references, and a cumulative subject index.

Hispanic American Voices presents full or excerpted speeches, sermons, orations, poems, testimony, and other notable spoken works of Hispanic Americans. Each entry is accompanied by an introduction and boxes explaining terms and events to which the speech refers. The volume contains pertinent black-and-white illustrations and a cumulative subject index.

Advisors

Special thanks are due for the invaluable comments and suggestions provided by U•X•L's Hispanic American books advisors:

Margarita Reichounia
Librarian, Bowen Branch
Detroit Public Library

Linda Garcia
Librarian, Southern Hills Middle School
Boulder, Colorado

Comments and Suggestions

We welcome your comments on *Hispanic American Biography* as well as your suggestions for topics to be featured in future editions. Please write: Editors, *Hispanic American Biography,* U•X•L, 835 Penobscot Bldg., Detroit, Michigan 48226-4094; call toll-free: 1-800-877-4253; or fax: 313-961-6348.

PICTURE CREDITS

The photographs and illustrations appearing in *Hispanic American Biography* were received from the following sources:

Cover: Sandra Cisneros: **AP/Wide World Photos;** Luis Valdez: **Arte Público Press;** Emiliano Zapata: **The Granger Collection, New York.**

Courtesy of Linda Alvarado: p. 1; **Photograph by Cynthia Farah:** p. 4; **AP/Wide World Photos:** pp. 7, 12, 15, 17, 19, 20, 32, 39, 43, 49, 51, 59, 62, 75, 77, 82, 90, 93, 95, 104, 109, 112, 125, 133, 140, 143, 151, 154, 163, 165, 169, 171, 179, 187, 194, 199, 201, 204, 220, 231; **Courtesy of Judith Baca:** p. 9; **The Granger Collection, New York:** pp. 23, 176, 229, 235; **UPI/Bettmann:** pp. 25, 212, 226; **Arte Público Press:** pp. 30, 64, 79, 88, 102, 107, 123, 135, 146, 149, 160, 173, 181, 192, 222, 224; **Archive Photos:** pp. 35, 183; **Photograph by Marty Sohl, courtesy of the San Francisco Ballet:** pp. 45, 46; **Photograph by Transcendental Graphics:** p. 54; **The Bettmann Archive:** pp. 56, 177, 209, 234; **©1993 Sony Music, courtesy of Epic Records:** p. 67; **Nancy Moran/Sygma:** p. 69; **Courtesy of José Feliciano:** p. 72; **Photograph by Helmut Newton:** p. 85; **Courtesy of Antonia Hernandez:** p. 97; **Bettmann Newsphotos:** p. 100; **Archive Photos/Kean Collection:** p. 119; **Courtesy of Aliza Lifshitz:** p. 121; **Courtesy of Wendy Lucero-Schayes:** p. 127; **Courtesy of Robert Martinez:** p. 137; **Courtesy of NASA:** p. 157; **Courtesy of Gloria Rodriguez:** p. 190; **National Catholic Reporter/Arthur Jones:** p. 197; **Courtesy of Cristina Saralegui:** p. 207; **Photograph by M. L. Marinelli, Publicity Department, Chronicle Books:** p. 215; **Courtesy of the U.S. Department of the Interior and the National Park Service:** p. 217.

Bartolomé de Las Casas

Missionary, historian
Born 1474, Seville, Spain
Died 1566, Madrid, Spain

"The more I thought about it the more convinced I was that everything we had done to the [native people] so far was nothing but tyranny and barbarism."

Bartolomé de Las Casas

For 50 years, Spanish missionary Bartolomé de Las Casas fought the inhumane treatment of the native people of the New World by Europeans through his writings, sermons, and example. Because of his efforts, laws were enacted to protect their rights, although many abuses continued. His book, *The Devastation of the Indies,* is an eyewitness account of life in the early Spanish settlements of the West Indies.

Not much is known about Las Casas's childhood. He was born sometime in 1474 in the city of Seville in southern Spain. His father, Pedro, was a merchant and his mother, who is thought to have been Isabel de Sosa, owned a bakery. It is known that his father and three of his uncles sailed on Christopher Columbus's second voyage to the New World in 1493. As a result, his father acquired some property in Hispaniola (an island in the present-day Caribbean Sea divided between the Dominican Republic on the east and Haiti on the west) and lived there for a while. During this period, Las Casas remained in Spain, studying theology and law at the University of Salamanca, northwest of the capital city of Madrid.

Joins Spanish Colonists on Hispaniola

By 1502 Las Casas had traveled to Hispaniola to live. The young man, fascinated by the native people of the island, studied their cultures and languages. Despite his understanding of the natives, he joined his fellow Spanish colonists in abusing them. Las Casas used the native Hispaniolans as slave workers to farm the land his father had given him. He saw nothing wrong with this practice.

The Spanish believed that Columbus had conquered Hispaniola and that the land and its people now belonged to Spain. Queen Isabella of Spain ordered the explorers to convert the natives to the Catholic faith and to teach them to read and to write. She also insisted that the native Hispaniolans be put to work to cure what she thought was their idleness. The explorers, however, were more interested in the gold and other treasures the New World had to offer than in converting the native people to the Catholic religion. In their greed for wealth, the explorers enslaved the natives to do the mining and the farming. Las Casas shared their desire for riches.

Disruption of the native Hispaniolan's hunting and food gathering practices—unchanged for thousands of years before the Spanish arrived on Hispaniola—caused famine among the tribes. Europeans brought diseases to the New World against which the native people had no natural defenses. Thousands died of smallpox, measles, and influenza. The natives tried to fight against this European invasion, but their primitive bows and arrows were no match for the swords the Spaniards wielded on horseback. Hundreds of thousands of natives died each year. Those who remained were quickly enslaved in their own lands.

Comes to New Understanding of Native People

Most Spaniards had no concept of the cultural and religious richness of the native Hispaniolans. They believed their treatment of the native people of the New World was morally correct—that it was, in fact, their religious duty to subdue and convert the "godless" natives to Christianity. Gradually, however, some recognized the suffering of the natives and began to speak out against the injustice. At first, Las Casas, who had been ordained a priest in 1512, was not sympathetic to those who spoke out. But in 1514, while reading a passage in the Bible, he experienced his own conversion. As he wrote later in his book, "The more I thought about it the more convinced I was that everything we had done to the [native people] so far was nothing but tyranny and barbarism."

Las Casas began to fight for the rights of native Hispaniolans. He gave up his land, freed his slaves, and began delivering angry sermons to the Spanish settlers. He also traveled back and forth to Spain to report to its rulers the injustices suffered by the native peoples.

In 1520 King Charles V of Spain granted Las Casas, who was now a bishop, some land to set up peaceful, free villages where native Hispaniolans could live and work with Spanish peasants. Under Las Casas's plan, the peasant families were to instruct the native people in European work as well as in Catholicism. The experiment quickly failed when the native Hispaniolans rebelled and the peasants deserted to join the other colonists. Las Casas was so discouraged that he returned to Spain and isolated himself in a monastery for nearly ten years.

Writings Bring About Change

During his stay at the monastery, Las Casas began working on his book, *The Devastation of the Indies: A Brief Account.* Published in 1542, it described the cruelties and tortures the Spanish had inflicted on native peoples since they had arrived in the New World. Europeans were shocked by the horrific stories of native women being raped in front of their husbands, of native children being thrown into rushing rivers, and of

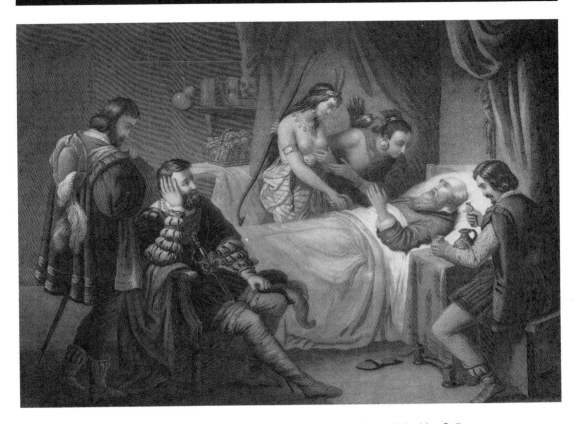

Affection of the Indians for Las Casas, an engraving by J. Hartman from original by Colin

young men being slowly burned alive. As a result, Charles V established the New Laws, which forbade the future enslavement of native Hispaniolans and gave guidelines for the proper treatment of those already working for Spanish landowners.

The settlers were outraged by these New Laws. While some returned to Spain rather than obey the laws, most simply disregarded them. Distance and the lack of communication between Spain and the New World hampered their enforcement. Under pressure, Charles V repealed the New Laws in 1545.

Las Casas continued to fight on behalf of native Hispaniolans for the rest of his life.

His book, translated into English, French, Dutch, German, and Italian, was read throughout Europe. For hundreds of years, the rest of Europe used the book to politically condemn Spain for its enslavement of the native peoples of the New World.

Those Europeans who came to colonize America did not embrace Las Casas's condemnation of all slavery. Earlier in his life, Las Casas had written that Africans should be substituted as slaves for native Hispaniolans because they were stronger. After he wrote his book, though, Las Casas changed his view, stating that enslavement of Africans was as unjust as enslavement of native

Hispaniolans. However, for hundreds of years some Americans used his earlier words to support their policy of slavery, choosing to ignore his later views.

For Further Information

America, July 18-25, 1992, pp. 30-32+.

Hanke, Lewis, *Bartolomé de Las Casas: Bookman, Scholar, and Propogandist,* University of Pennsylvania Press, 1952.

Las Casas, Bartolomé de, *The Devastation of the Indies: A Brief Account,* translated by Hans Magnus Enzenberger, Seabury Press, 1974.

Wagner, Henry Raup, *The Life and Writings of Bartolomé de Las Casas,* University of New Mexico Press, 1967.

Aliza Lifshitz

Doctor, reporter
Born c. 1947, Mexico City, Mexico

"I would basically like in some way to leave this world a little bit better than what I found it."

A liza Lifshitz's patients call her an old-fashioned doctor who listens to them and takes the time to explain medical terms. Yet she is also a physician who skillfully uses the media to educate Hispanic television viewers and readers on present-day advances in health and medicine. In 1992 she served as the president of the California Hispanic American Medical Association, which has 1,300 members. She was also one of the first Hispanic woman physicians to become actively involved in the struggle against AIDS.

Lifshitz was born in Mexico City, Mexico, sometime in the late 1940s. Her Jewish father was an engineer and a classical pianist; her Mexican mother was an artist. Her parents enrolled her in the American elementary school in Mexico City so she could experience cultural diversity and learn English. She then attended both Jewish and Catholic schools. After having graduated from high school, Lifshitz enrolled in the Colegio Israelite de Mexico, earning her bachelor's degree with honors in 1969.

Healing Through Communication

Lifshitz decided she wanted a career that would allow her to be both creative and helpful to others. She chose medicine. "I've always seen medicine as an art that is based on a science," she explained to Diana Martínez in *Notable Hispanic American Women.* "The greatest majority of the healing that we do is actually through listening to the patient and communicating with them." Lifshitz enrolled in the Universidad Nacional Autonoma de México. After she graduated in 1976, she completed her medical training in the United States at the University of California at San Diego.

As a physician specializing in internal medicine, Lifshitz has worked with community-based organizations to make sure poor patients receive the treatment they need. She has been paid with knitting, handmade decorations, cookies, and fruit. She says she truly enjoys helping her patients and is happy with whatever they bring her.

Many of Lifshitz's patients admire her for her compassion. She attributes this trait to her parents, especially to her mother. "My mother had a tremendously big heart for people," Lifshitz told Martínez. "I remember her taking care of everything from a limping dog on the street to making sure she bought food for people who she saw needed it. That's what my mother was all about."

Explores Health Issues Through the Media

In 1986 Lifshitz appeared on a live, 30-minute call-in program on a southern California television station. After receiving and answering hundreds of calls, she realized she could reach out to many more people in her community through the media than through her office practice alone. Since that time, she has become the health reporter for Univision, a Spanish-language television network in Los Angeles. She is also the medical editor of *Más,* a national Spanish-language magazine, and editor-in-chief of *Hispanic Physician.*

One of the main issues Lifshitz focuses on through her media outlets is the lack of information available to the Hispanic community regarding AIDS (Acquired Immune Deficiency Syndrome) and HIV (Human Immunodeficiency Virus, which results in AIDS). "In very many instances it has been said ... that Hispanics are not interested in preventive health," she explained to Martínez. "But many times it's simply because Hispanics don't have access to that information. Once data are made available to them, they are very interested." Lifshitz devotes about one-third of her practice to the treatment of patients who are HIV-positive.

Lifshitz is also concerned with the need for universal health care. "We need to be able to provide basic health care for everyone in

Aliza Lifshitz

a country that is supposed to be a developed country," she pointed out to Martínez. "If we are going to rate how civilized a country is according to how they treat their poor, I think we're becoming more and more uncivilized." In addition, Lifshitz believes more attention should be paid especially to women's health issues and to the position of women in medicine. Lifshitz notes that women have made significant contributions to health care—beyond traditional nursing—that the world should readily recognize.

Lifshitz has received numerous honors for her work in educating the public on health matters. In 1992 the University of Southern California Los Amigos De La Humanidad of the School of Social Work bestowed its Distinguished Contributor to Social Welfare award on her. Lifshitz is motivated in her hard-working efforts by one strong desire, as she explained to Martínez: "I would basically like in some way to leave this world a little bit better than what I found it."

For Further Information

Hispanic, October 1991, p. 15.
Notable Hispanic American Women, Gale Research, 1993, pp. 229-31.
Unidos, April 1992, pp. 16-18.

Nancy Lopez

Professional golfer
Born January 6, 1957, Torrance, California

"I've always felt like a role model for the Hispanic people. I hope that I stand for honesty."

Nancy Lopez is one of the youngest women golfers to achieve professional success. Since 1978, she has consistently ranked among the top women players. She is one of only five women in the sport to have earned more than $1 million in her career. In addition, she has won over 40 tournament victories. In 1987 she became the youngest woman ever to be named to the Ladies Professional Golf Association (LPGA) Hall of Fame.

Lopez was born in 1957 in Torrance, California, but raised in Roswell, New Mexico. She learned to play golf when her parents, Domingo and Marina Lopez, took up the game for her mother's health. By the age of 11, she was a better golfer than either of her parents, and her father was convinced that she should pursue the sport as a career. The family tried to scrape up the money to pay for her lessons and practice. However, the Lopezes were hindered not only by finances but also by prejudice. "My dad worked so hard to do so much for me," she recounted to Annette Alvarez in *Hispanic,* "and a lot of doors were shut in our faces because he couldn't afford to get me into the country club so I could play golf there."

Perseverance Brings Early Success

Lopez's struggle against these barriers quickly paid off. At the age of 12, she won the New Mexico Women's Open. She then went on to become the only female member of her high school golf team. In 1972 and 1974, she won the U.S. Girls Junior title, and while still in high school placed second in the U.S. Women's Open golf tournament. She won a golf scholarship to the University of Tulsa, where she won the intercollegiate golf title before dropping out to turn professional.

Her first year of professional play—1978—was a whirlwind for Lopez. She broke several records and won nine tournaments, including the famed Ladies Professional Golf Association (LPGA) title. It was her year for collecting trophies—she was named Rookie of the Year, Player of the Year, Golfer of the Year, and Female Athlete of the Year. She also set a new record for earnings by a rookie, winning over $200,000.

Dominates Her Sport

Lopez continued to mow down her opponents the following year. She won eight more tournaments, which brought her two-year-old career victory total to 17. It was a feat Bruce Newman of *Sports Illustrated* called "one of the most dominating sports performances in half a century." Lopez proved she was a true sports superstar by continuing to overshadow many of her fellow golfers during the 1980s. Her best year was 1985—her eighth on the pro circuit. That year she won five tournaments and earned over $400,000

Lopez began balancing the demands of her sports career with the role of wife and, later, mother when she married New York Mets third baseman Ray Knight in 1982. Over the years, the couple has had three daughters: Ashley, Erinn, and Torri. Many sports writers and observers have marveled at what has come be called a model marriage. Lopez explained to Jaime Diaz of *Sports Illustrated* that her marriage to Knight has given her peace of mind. "I'm so happy with my life, that now when I play, there is no pressure. It's just all fun, and when it's fun, you perform better."

Happiness at home indeed seemed to enhance Lopez's career. In 1987 she was named to the LPGA Hall of Fame. The LPGA has some of the most difficult requirements for entry of any sports Hall of Fame: nominees must have 30 tournament victories, of which two must be major titles. By the end of 1987, Lopez had passed the $2 million mark in golf-related earnings. That same year she also authored a book, *Nancy Lopez's the Complete Golfer.*

Focus Extends Beyond Golf

Lopez has achieved greatness in her career through hard work and self-discipline.

Nancy Lopez

Yet she has never forgotten that any sport is meant to be fun, and she has maintained a cheerful and positive approach. As Alvarez noted, "Lopez has a tremendous following because, regardless of how busy she is, Lopez will find time to give an autograph, do an interview, pose for pictures, give a smile, and shake hands."

As her family has grown, so has Lopez's commitment to issues outside the golfing world. When she can, she volunteers her time to Aid for the Handicapped, an organization that helps children with physical disabilities. And she has never forgotten her community and the hardships she overcame as a child. "I've always felt like a role model for the Hispanic people," she told Alvarez. "I hope that I stand for honesty." Her status as a role model was confirmed in 1991 when the Roswell, New Mexico, school board changed the name of Flora Vista Elementary School (her old school) to Nancy Lopez Elementary School.

For Further Information

Hispanic, June 1989, pp. 15-16.

Lopez, Nancy, *Nancy Lopez's the Complete Golfer,* Contemporary Books, 1987.

Sports Illustrated, August 4, 1986, p. 34-35+; February 9, 1987, pp. 84-85.

Women's Sports and Fitness, August 1985, pp. 15-16.

Los Lobos

Mexican American roots/rock band

"At the heart of the Los Lobos sound is the traditional music of their Mexican parents and grandparents and the mainstream pop music they grew up with in the 1960s."—Mark Holston, Hispanic

Los Lobos reached commercial stardom in 1987 when they recorded the successful soundtrack for the film La Bamba, which retold the life story of Mexican American singer Ritchie Valens (see **Ritchie Valens**). The band had been together for 14 years before that, combining country swing, rock and roll, Mexican folk songs, and rhythm and blues into a sound that is both old and new. "At the heart of the Los Lobos sound," Mark Holston wrote in *Hispanic,* "is the traditional music of their Mexican parents and grandparents and the mainstream pop music they grew up with in the 1960s."

The four original members of Los Lobos—David Hidalgo, Cesar Rosas, Louie Pérez, and Conrad Lozano—have known each other since their high school days in the same Los Angeles area neighborhood. Until 1973 they had all played in various bands. Tired of playing Top 40 songs over and over, they decided to join together to explore their Mexican roots and to learn the folk songs they had once taken for granted.

Folk Music

Taking the name Los Lobos (Spanish for "the wolves"), the members collected as many old recordings of Mexican folk music as they could find. They then studied each song carefully in order to play it properly. Many of the songs required instruments—such as the *vihuela,* a sixteenth-century Spanish guitar similar to the lute—that the members of the group had never even played before. They started playing at parties, weddings, and other small events. They landed their first full-time professional job in 1978 at a Mexican restaurant in Orange County in California.

"It wasn't even a real Mexican restaurant," Rosas told an interviewer in *Guitar World.* "One of those tourist joints. We were working there because we had come to a point where we had to either make more money from music or find other jobs; some of us had gotten married, and we weren't kids anymore."

For their first eight years, Los Lobos were an all-acoustic group playing only traditional music. The members had accumulated over 30 different folk and classical instruments, taking time to learn how to use each one properly. They then began adding other instruments, like the accordion, and their

Los Lobos

own electric guitars and amplifiers. Their two-year job at the restaurant ended when the owner complained that their music had become too loud.

In 1978 the group had also recorded its first album, *Just Another Band from East L.A.* Financed by the members themselves, the album sold poorly. After a while, they decided to try recording again, but this time with their own material. As Los Lobos's songs were heard more and more around Los Angeles, their reputation grew until they signed a recording contract with Slash/ Warner Bros. Their musical hobby quickly became more serious. In 1983 they released a recording called *...And A Time To Dance.* Music critics praised it. A song off the album, "Anselma," won a Grammy award for best Mexican American performance.

Extensive Musical Ability

The members of Los Lobos have an impressive range of musical ability. From the very beginning, instead of hiring additional musicians to play the different instruments, the four members split the instruments among themselves. Pérez had begun playing drums only years after he joined the group. He was originally a guitarist, having picked up the instrument when he was 12. In his mid-twenties, he was elected to play drums when Los Lobos began to go electric. Pérez, along with Hidalgo, also writes most of the group's songs.

Hidalgo began playing guitar when he was 11. He launched his career as a drummer in the early 1970s by playing in a Christian rock band. He also plays violin, accordion, and drums. "You have to understand, the group does work and evolve around David," Lozano said of Hidalgo in *Musician.* "His playing is so strong; his talent is still being tapped."

Lozano, who plays both electric and acoustic bass, began playing rock and roll when he was 16. He juggled his time between two bands before jumping to Los Lobos in 1973. Rosas is from Sonora, Mexico. He immigrated to Los Angeles with his family when he was 7. Basically a self-taught guitar player, he took some lessons in order to learn chords and musical theory. He also plays the mandolin and the vihuela.

Steve Berlin joined the group in the early 1980s after working on one of their recordings. His full tenor and baritone saxes add another dimension to Los Lobos's sound. Berlin also coproduced the group's first full-length album, *How Will the Wolf Survive?* Released in 1984, the highly acclaimed record features a wide variety of styles, from Tex-Mex polkas to New Orleans rhythm and blues.

Los Lobos's follow-up album, *By The Light of the Moon,* released in 1987, showed the group's superb musicianship and featured songs whose lyrics offered social commentary. That same year, Los Lobos recreated the original recordings of the late Ritchie Valens for the movie *La Bamba.* Many thought their recreations were better than the originals, and their version of the title track reached number one on the popular music charts. The soundtrack album also spent two weeks at number one. The group's new audience stretched across the country.

The instant popularity, however, almost proved to be too much for the band. "That kind of eclipsed everything else we had done up to that point," Pérez explained in *Time.* "[But] we didn't know if we were going to

be an alternative novelty thing or just a flavor of the month."

To remain centered, the members of Los Lobos returned to what was most important to them—the folk songs of their youth. In 1988 they released *La Pistola y El Corazón,* an album composed wholly of those folk songs. The recording earned the group its second Grammy award. A *Guitar World* critic described the album as "a stunning personal statement of musical faith by a band at the height of its creative powers."

Since that time, Los Lobos has continued to bridge the gap between mainstream American music and its Mexican roots. *The Neighborhood* (1990) and *Kiko* (1992) showcased their smooth blend of rock, jazz, and Mexican folk songs. Other prominent musicians, like Ry Cooder and Paul Simon, have tapped Los Lobos's talents for various projects of their own. In 1992 the group also lent its sound to the recording for *The Mambo Kings,* the film adaptation of the Pulitzer Prize-winning novel by Oscar Hijuelos (see **Oscar Hijuelos**). The following year the band released another album called *Just Another Band from East L.A.* The 20-year anniversary career retrospective generated tremendous excitement among fans and the musical community.

For Further Information

Guitar World, September 1986; February 1989.
Hispanic, March 1994, p. 48.
Musician, April 1987.
Time, November 26, 1990, pp. 88-89.

Wendy Lucero-Schayes

Broadcaster, former Olympic athlete
Born June 26, 1963, Denver, Colorado

"The success I've had in sports overcoming those people who didn't think that I could [succeed] has made me like myself better.... Hopefully I can share that with others."

Wendy Lucero-Schayes

When she was a young girl, Wendy Lucero-Schayes dreamed of being an Olympic athlete. She trained as a gymnast and as a figure skater before finally settling on diving. She was a member of the U.S. Diving National Team for eight years. During that time, she won nine national titles, three U.S. Olympic Festival titles, and several medals in international competition. In 1988 she competed in the summer Olympics in Seoul, Korea. She then went on to begin a career in television broadcasting.

Lucero-Schayes was born in 1963 in Denver, Colorado, to Dan and Shirley Lucero. Her father, the son of Spanish immigrants, worked as an electrician. Her mother, of Irish heritage, worked at home, raising the three Lucero children. Growing up in an athletic family, Lucero-Schayes began swimming and dancing at an early age. She later learned gymnastics, tennis, and diving while tagging along to her older sister's lessons.

Sports soon became an activity at which the tomboy Lucero-Schayes excelled. Part of the motivation behind her success was her fierce desire to compete against her older sister. "I would always strive to be the best I could be," Lucero-Schayes explained to Diane Telgen in *Notable Hispanic American Women,* "because I wanted to grasp what my sister was attaining—but I wanted it now, even though I was two years younger."

Skating Star Inspires Dream

Lucero-Schayes first dreamed of competing in the Olympics when she was nine years old. She thought she would compete in gymnastics, but soon realized that her late start in the sport would severely limit her chance of success. After watching Dorothy Hamill win the gold medal in figure skating in the 1976 winter games in Innsbruck, Austria, Lucero-Schayes was inspired to become a skater. After competing for four years, however, she again realized that she had begun the sport too late. In addition, her family did not have the finances necessary for her to compete nationally.

In high school, Lucero-Schayes returned to the sport of diving. Her gymnastics training helped her excel at springboard events. At the end of her senior year in high school, she competed in the Junior Olympic Championships, finishing sixth in the three-meter event. For her success in this competition and others that year, she was named 1981's Hispanic Athlete of the Year. Cited as an Academic All-American, she received a scholarship to the University of Nebraska.

Lucero-Schayes's parents placed a high value on education. They encouraged her to work hard at her studies, as well as at diving. After two years at the University of Nebraska, Lucero-Schayes transferred to Southern Illinois University, where she had more chances to compete on a national level. She won the 1985 National Collegiate Athletic Association championship and earned her first national titles. She was also named an Academic All-American for her performance in the classroom.

Even then, Lucero-Schayes wanted to be more than just a diver. After earning her bachelor's degree in 1986 in television sales and management, she sought out opportunities in broadcasting and television production. "As I was training for the Olympic Games in 1988 and the few years before that," she related to Telgen, "I would try to be a production assistant for golf tournaments, horse tournaments, Monday Night Football—anything I could do." She worked as a sportscaster for television networks and hosted a talk show, "Focus Colorado," in her hometown of Denver.

Olympic Training Marred by Mother's Illness

Lucero-Schayes encountered two problems during her training for the 1988 U.S. Olympic trials. First, her mother, who had always encouraged her, developed breast cancer and had to undergo chemotherapy treatments. Second, her coach undermined her self-confidence, telling her she probably would not make the Olympics. Lucero-Schayes switched coaches and focused on training for her mother's sake.

Lucero-Schayes's mother soon recovered and was able to watch her daughter compete in the trials. Lucero-Schayes was greatly motivated by the presence of her mother. She turned in one of the best performances of her career and finished second, qualifying for the U.S. Olympic team. Her victory was especially sweet because she had beaten competitors who were guided by her former coach.

At the 1988 Summer Olympics in Seoul, Lucero-Schayes finished sixth. Although she didn't win a medal, she enjoyed the experience of meeting and competing against other athletes from around the world. After Olympic competition, Lucero-Schayes continued her work in communications. She increased her involvement in public speaking, visiting schools and speaking at charity events and conferences. She served as a spokesperson for the American Cancer Society, and often appeared as a motivational speaker in front of groups, passing on what she has learned. "The success I've had in sports overcoming those people who didn't think that I could [succeed] has made me like myself better.... Hopefully I can share that with others," she related to Telgin.

Lucero-Schayes met her husband, professional basketball player Dan Schayes, at a charity benefit where they both spoke. Finding sports to be a bond, they married in 1991. They not only train together but also give each other understanding and support during the stress and strain of competition.

U.S. Female Diving Athlete of the Year

1991 was a banner year for Lucero-Schayes. In the national indoor championships that year, she placed first in both the one-meter and the three-meter springboard events. In the outdoor championships, she won the one-meter event and placed second in the three-meter event. At the Sixth World Championship and at the Alamo International competition, she received silver medals. At the end of the 1991 season, Lucero-Schayes was voted the U.S. Female Diving Athlete of the Year (she had also won the award the previous year).

A severe intestinal infection kept Lucero-Schayes from training properly for the 1992 U.S. Olympic trials. At the competition, she finished third—one place short of qualifying for her second Olympic team. Her greatest disappointment was in not having the chance to compete in Barcelona, Spain, the country of her ancestors. Overall, Lucero-Schayes was still satisfied with a sporting career that paid for her college education and enabled her to travel around the world.

Lucero-Schayes's long-term plans include returning to Denver to continue her work in communications. Her athletic career over, she hopes to inspire others through a different medium, as she explained to Telgin: "I always felt that communications—whether radio and television, or through newspapers and journalism—it's going to shape our world, it is the up-and-coming future."

For Further Information

Atlanta Constitution, July 28, 1989, p. F3; August 2, 1990. p. F7.
Detroit Free Press, April 14, 1992, p. D1.
Notable Hispanic American Women, Gale, 1993, pp. 242-45.

Manuel Lujan, Jr.

Utilities executive, retired congressional representative, former secretary of the U.S. Department of the Interior
Born May 12, 1928, San Ildefonso, New Mexico

"Lujan's term as the secretary of the U.S. Department of the Interior was marked by considerable controversy."

In 1968 Manuel Lujan, Jr., became the first Hispanic Republican elected to the U.S. House of Representatives. For 20 years, Lujan served quietly in the House as a representative of the state of New Mexico, working on issues that best benefited those people in his home district. In 1988 he decided to retire from politics, but then--president-elect George Bush convinced Lujan to become a member of his cabinet. Lujan's term as the secretary of the U.S. Department of the Interior was marked by considerable controversy. Many environmentalists disagreed with almost all of his

Manuel Lujan, Jr.

married Jean Kay Couchman; the couple eventually had four children.

Following one year at St. Mary's, Lujan transferred to the College of Santa Fe, where he earned his bachelor's degree in business administration in 1950. After college, he helped run his father's business. In the early 1960s, he became active in politics, serving for a while as vice chairman of New Mexico's Republican party. Lujan ran for the representative's seat in New Mexico's First Congressional District in 1968. He appealed to the district's Hispanic voters, who normally voted Democratic, and was elected. While serving as a representative, Lujan worked mostly on measures that directly affected his constituents. He was re-elected by overwhelming margins throughout his 20 years in Congress. His only serious threat came in the early 1980s, when he was accused by his Democratic opponents of voting on issues that benefited his family's insurance business.

Poor Environmental Record in Congress

Beginning in 1969, Lujan served on the House Interior and Insular Affairs Committee, which handles issues regarding the nation's natural resources. His work on the committee, however, earned him low marks with environmentalists. He cosponsored a bill that would have allowed oil and gas companies to begin drilling in the Arctic National Wildlife Refuge. This ecologically sensitive area in northeast Alaska is America's largest wildlife refuge. In addition, he voted to support the nuclear power industry while cutting federal energy conservation funds. He did, however, vote in 1987 to

wildlife and wilderness policies and believed his programs damaged the very lands he was supposed to protect.

Lujan was born in 1928 in San Ildefonso, a small town on the Rio Grande River in northern New Mexico. He was the eighth of Manuel and Lorenzita Romero Lujan's eleven children. His father, who owned a successful insurance agency, had served three terms as the mayor of the nearby city of Santa Fe.

While growing up in San Ildefonso, Lujan attended parochial schools (private schools run by churches or other religious organizations). He graduated from high school in 1948, then enrolled in St. Mary's College in San Francisco. In November of that year he

override President Ronald Reagan's veto of a clean water bill.

President Reagan, who served from 1981 to 1988, twice considered Lujan for the top spot in the Department of the Interior but passed him over both times. In 1988, at the end of his tenth term in Congress, Lujan decided to retire. He believed he had served long enough. President-elect Bush, however, thought Lujan would be perfect for the Interior Department position. "Manuel knows the issues," Bush said, as quoted by Bruce Reed in the *New Republic*. At first, lacking interest, Lujan declined the job. Only after Bush personally appealed to him did Lujan accept the offer.

The Department of the Interior is responsible for managing almost 450 million acres of wilderness in the United States. The department also directs the Bureau of Land Management and the National Parks Service. The job of the secretary of the interior is to balance environmental protection with the need for the development of natural resources. As energy needs have increased and energy sources have declined over the past decades, the secretary's balancing act has become harder and harder to manage.

Questions Nation's Environmental Policies

The day after he was sworn in as secretary of the interior, Lujan proposed that oil companies be allowed to explore in the Arctic National Wildlife Refuge. From the beginning, Lujan questioned the need for the strict Endangered Species Act, which was passed by Congress in 1973. He did not think it was necessary for every type of animal to be protected over the needs of industry. "Nobody's told me the difference between a red squirrel, a black one, or a brown one," Lujan said, according to Ted Gup of *Time*.

Environmentalists believed Lujan was ill-suited for his job. Many thought he knew nothing about the situation facing endangered species and wilderness areas. One example was his lack of concern about wetlands, where almost half of all endangered species live. While biologists and other experts have found it difficult to define exactly what wetlands are, Lujan offered a simple approach. "I take the position that there are certain kinds of vegetation that are common in wetlands—pussy willows or whatever the name is." Gup quoted him as saying. "That's one way you can tell. [Another is] if it's wet."

As secretary, Lujan did introduce a number of measures that almost everyone agreed with. He helped upgrade schools on Native American reservations (Native American lands fall under the jurisdiction of the Department of the Interior), protected historical battlefields that were threatened by developers, and raised the government's earnings from private food stands in federal parks. He also increased the number of minorities hired by the Department of the Interior.

Speeches Land Him in Trouble

What angered many people, however, were Lujan's seemingly inappropriate public remarks on environmental issues. One instance occurred after the *Exxon Valdez* oil spill in March of 1989. The environmental disaster was the worst in American history. The tanker spilled 11 million gallons of oil into Prince William Sound, off the southern coastline of Alaska, killing much wildlife and threatening to destroy the area's fishing industry. Lujan appeared on Alaskan television a few months after the incident and compared it to the massive fires that had destroyed much of Yellowstone National Park the previous year. "If the same experience holds true for Alaska that held for Yellowstone," he said rather sarcastically, as quoted by Reed, "your tourism should increase this year."

During his four years as secretary of the interior, Lujan claimed that he tried to maintain a balance between environmental concerns and economic development. After Bill Clinton defeated Bush in the 1992 U.S. presidential race, Bruce Babbitt was named the new secretary of the Department of the Interior. In April of 1994 Lujan became a director of the Public Service Company of New Mexico, a utility company based in Albuquerque.

For Further Information

New Republic, October 16, 1989, pp. 20-22.
Time, May 25, 1992, pp. 57-59.
Wall Street Journal, April 12, 1994, p. B8.

Sonia Manzano

Actress, writer
Born June 12, 1950, New York, New York

"I think it has a terrible impact when you don't see yourself reflected in the society because then you get the feeling you don't exist."

While she was growing up in the United States, Sonia Manzano never saw any Hispanic images in children's books or in the media. Today things are very different—thanks in part to Manzano. She portrays the character "Maria" on the long-running, award-winning children's show *Sesame Street.* Manzano thinks her character, beyond being a positive role model, is important for Hispanic children across the country simply because she exists. "I think it has a terrible impact when you don't see yourself reflected in the society," she explained to Luis Vasquez-Ajmac in *Notable Hispanic American Women,* "because then you get the feeling you don't exist."

Manzano was born in New York City in 1950. She is one of four children born to Bonifacio Manzano, a roofer, and Isidra Rivera, a seamstress. Of Puerto Rican descent, Manzano was raised in the South Bronx (a section of New York City) as part of a very close-knit, Spanish-speaking community.

Manzano never thought of pursuing a career in show business until she was a junior in high school. With the encouragement of a teacher, Manzano went to the famous High School for the Performing Arts in New York City. After graduating, she earned a scholarship to attend Carnegie Mellon University in Pittsburgh, Pennsylvania. There she majored in drama.

How She Got to Sesame Street

While in college, Manzano was cast in the musical *Godspell.* She was later part of the original cast when the popular play came to Broadway. A theatrical agent noticed her talent during one of her *Godspell* performances and helped her win an audition for a role on *Sesame Street*.

When Manzano began working on *Sesame Street* in 1972, the emphasis of the TV series was on helping black inner-city children. With its endearing muppet characters, fast pace, and catchy tunes, the program was so appealing that preschool children of almost every ethnic group across the nation began to watch it. The quick humor, original presentation, and educational themes made *Sesame Street* a favorite of parents, as well. With the addition of the character "Maria," Manzano introduced a new role model for Hispanic children.

Maria was a teenager when Manzano took on the role. The character has grown and changed quite a bit over the years. Manzano has portrayed her through various stages—from a hippie to a radical feminist. She has also taken Maria through a courtship and into a marriage.

After having portrayed the outspoken, warmhearted, multitalented Maria for ten years, Manzano began writing scripts for the show. She hoped to make her character more visible and realistic, and to help erase racial-ethnic stereotypes. Manzano also wanted to blend Hispanic culture into the story lines. She often wrote material based on her own real-life experiences.

Maria's Baby

Along with numbers, letters, and social skills, *Sesame Street* has taught American children about life. Kids learned about families when Maria and fellow character "Luis" married on the show in 1988. When Manzano became pregnant in real life, writers

Sonia Manzano

included the pregnancy in Maria's story line. As Manzano pointed out to *Newsweek*'s Jean Seligmann, the pregnancy "gave us an opportunity to deal with something kids really face." By watching the show, children learned how a fetus develops, eats, and breathes inside a mother, and how a mother's body changes during pregnancy. They also heard the baby's heartbeat and watched the parents prepare for its arrival in 1989. Manzano's own child plays the couple's baby.

Manzano has earned seven Emmy awards as a member of the *Sesame Street* writing staff. In 1991 she won an award from the Hispanic Congressional Caucus in Washington, D.C. Manzano has no interest in leaving *Sesame Street*. She is very content acting and writing for the top-rated children's show. By enriching children's lives and expressing her ideas, Manzano believes that she has been a positive influence. Married since 1986, Manzano especially enjoys working with her own daughter, Gabriela, on *Sesame Street.*

For Further Information

Children Today,, September/October 1989, pp. 20-22.
Newsweek, May 15, 1989, p. 71.
Notable Hispanic American Women, Gale Research, 1993, pp. 249-250.

José Martí

Cuban revolutionary, writer, journalist
Born January 28, 1853, Havana, Cuba
Died May 19, 1895, Dos Rios, Cuba

"Freedom is dearly bought and either we resign ourselves to living without it or we resolve to have it at its price."

José Martí was a Cuban poet and patriot who led a revolution on his island homeland during the 1800s. Banished from Cuba because of his political beliefs, he lived in Spain, Mexico, and the United States, using his writings to raise support for the cause of his people. Throughout his time in exile, he always passionately planned to return to Cuba. Martí championed understanding and respect between cultures, and gave his life for freedom.

Martí was born José Julián Martí y Pérez, the son of a retired Spanish army sergeant. The elder Martí worked as a night watchman to supplement his army pension, but his earnings were barely enough to provide his family with the bare necessities. Despite growing up in poverty, Martí became an excellent student. At the age of four, he traveled with his parents to Spain where he began his education. After he returned to Cuba in 1859, he completed his primary education. He then was admitted to the prestigious Institute of Havana, a college "prep" school.

Cuba had been a Spanish-controlled colony since the 1500s, and for over 300 years slavery existed on the island. During the 1860s, many Cuban intellectuals began to call for social reforms and complete political independence. From the time he was a young boy, Martí had seen the brutality of slavery. Despite his father's continued loyalty to Spain, he soon joined the growing revolt against Spanish rule. By the age of 16, he was writing articles and poems critical of the Spanish government and helping to edit a new journal, *La Patria Libre* ("The Free Homeland"). Outspoken and defiant, he eventually came to the attention of the intolerant police. He was arrested for disloyalty, sentenced to six months of hard labor, then deported to Spain.

Studies Law and Starts a Family

While in Spain, Martí earned literature and law degrees and became even more committed to Cuban independence. He wrote a pamphlet about the suffering of Cubans to motivate the people of Spain to bring about changes in their government's control of Cuba. In 1875 he moved to Mexico to work as a journalist, submitting political articles to newspapers. He traveled to Guatemala two years later and was made a professor of literature at the Central School.

All the while, he continued writing essays and articles on behalf of Cuban independence and working with other Latin American reformers to bring about change. While in Guatemala, he met and married Maria Garcia Granados.

By 1878 the authorities had gained control over the revolt in Cuba. For the moment, peace returned to the island. Accompanied by his new wife, Martí returned to Cuba hoping to practice law. Government officials still considered him dangerous, however, and would neither grant him a law license nor allow him to teach. While Martí struggled to find work, his wife gave birth to their son, Ismael. To support his new family, he turned to his writing. Once again, his anti-government views led Cuban leaders to deport him to Spain. After just two months in Spain, Martí traveled to New York City.

Moves to U.S. and Plans Invasion

Many exiled Cubans lived in New York, and Martí joined with them to gather support from Americans for a rebellion against Spain. Martí longed for a nonviolent solution to Cuba's problems. During the 1880s he was extremely busy working toward that end. His articles calling for Cuban independence appeared in leading Latin American newspapers such as *La Opinión Nacional* of Caracas and *La Nación* of Buenos Aires, Argentina. His writings made him well known throughout North and South America. In 1881 Martí went to Venezuela to work for the renowned newspaper *Revista Venezolana*. His political articles, though, were deemed too radical by the country's dictator, Antonio Guzmán Blanco, and Martí

José Martí

was forced to leave Venezuela after only five months.

Upon his return to New York, Martí continued to submit articles to American newspapers. Not all of his writings, however, were political. He wrote a Spanish magazine for children and became editor of New York's Spanish-language newspaper, *La America*. He not only translated Spanish works for New York publishers, but also translated into Spanish the works of such American writers as the essayist Ralph Waldo Emerson and the poet Walt Whitman. His writing output was tremendous and included novels and poems that were highly praised by literary critics. Believing poetry was only successful if it could be understood by everyone, Martí developed a clear poetic style. His best-known volume of poems, *Versos sencillos* ("Simple Verses"), published in 1891, focused on the themes of love and friendship. By the early 1890s, Martí was perhaps the most famous Latin American writer.

Even though Martí's experiences in Mexico, Guatemala, Venezuela, and the United States led him to work toward Hispanic unity and solidarity, his commitment to Cuban independence remained strong. In 1892 he stopped all his other activities to concentrate fully on organizing a revolution. He founded the Cuban Revolutionary party. A rousing speaker, Martí urged Cubans and Puerto Ricans in the United States to join him or contribute to the cause. In 1895 he launched a carefully planned invasion of Cuba from the coast of Florida. Once in Cuba, he was named Major General of the Army of Liberation. His followers feared for his safety and tried to convince him to return to the United States to continue to gain support for their cause. Prepared to die for independence, Martí would not leave his homeland again.

Martí's Name Lives on in Cuba Today

On May 19, 1895, Martí rode into a battle on a white horse and was shot down. The 42-year-old leader was one of the first to die in the revolution that, three years later, gained Cuba its freedom from Spain. He is credited with making the free world aware of Cuba's problems and gaining the support and help of the United States in its fight. His political writings and stories of immigrant life in New York are still quoted and studied today.

Many Cuban Americans consider Martí to be the author of the revolution that is still being fought today against the Communist government of Fidel Castro. In 1982 Cuban Americans won approval for the creation of a Voice of America radio station that beams news and music from the United States to Cuba. Television transmissions followed in 1990. Organizers honored Martí by naming the stations Radio Marti and TV Marti.

For Further Information

American History Illustrated, July/August 1990, pp. 56-9+.

Appel, Todd M., *José Martí,* Chelsea House, 1992.

Gray, Richard Butler, *José Martí: Cuban Patriot,* University of Florida Press, 1962.

Kirk, John M., *José Martí: Mentor of the Cuban Nation,* University Presses of Florida, 1983.

Martí, José, *Major Poems,* translated by Elinor Randall, edited by Philip S. Foner, Holmes & Meier, 1982.

Robert Martínez

Director of the Office of National Drug Control Policy, former governor of Florida
Born December 25, 1934, Tampa, Florida

"Martínez came in and scared the hell out of everybody. As it ended up, he was a great mayor."—Phil Lewis, Miami Herald

Robert Martínez is a public figure who is used to conflict and harsh criticism. His no-nonsense, firm style of leadership has angered some and pleased others during his work as a teacher, business owner, mayor, and governor. In 1991 he became director of the Office of National Drug Control Policy. As director, he is responsible for developing a nationwide plan for stopping the use of illegal drugs. In this high-level government position, he has received some of his heaviest criticism.

Martínez was born in Tampa, Florida, on Christmas Day in 1934 to a third-generation Spanish-American family. His father, Serafin, worked as a waiter. His mother, Ida, was a garment worker. His parents did not have much money, but managed to send him to the University of Tampa. Trained as a social studies teacher, he graduated in 1957, married, and found a teaching job in Tampa.

Martínez and his wife, Mary Jane, soon had two children. Realizing he would need to earn more money to support his family, Martínez returned to college to study labor and industrial relations. After he received his master's degree from the University of Illinois in 1964, he returned to his original teaching position in Tampa. He was then elected director of the local teachers' union and went on to write its first contract in 1966. Two years later he earned his reputation as a fighter when he ignored the contract he had just written and led his group in a teachers' strike.

In 1975 Martínez left the union and his teaching job to take over his uncle's Spanish restaurant, the Café Sevilla. Running the restaurant was a demanding job that kept him busy 17 hours a day, seven days a week. Martínez admitted later that the hard work was great training for politics. In an effort to promote the restaurant, he got involved with the local Chamber of Commerce (an organization of local business owners).

Robert Martínez

Runs for Mayor of Tampa

His close contact with the Chamber of Commerce increased his involvement with city issues. In 1979 he decided to run for mayor of Tampa. He was successful. The city was in sad economic shape, but Martínez's experience with unions made him a tough leader. "Martínez came in and scared the hell out of everybody," former Florida State Senate president Phil Lewis told a *Miami Herald* reporter. "As it ended up, he was a great mayor."

Once when Martínez was holding a meeting with political supporters at his restaurant, the kitchen staff announced they were striking for higher wages. Martínez excused himself from the table, walked into the kitchen, and fired the entire staff. He then tied on an apron and did his best to prepare the night's meals.

As mayor of Tampa, Martínez tackled labor disputes in much the same manner. When the city's sanitation workers objected to working conditions, he fired the whole department. He then replaced many of the fired workers with automatic machinery. Labor leaders were angered by his moves, but Martínez responded that he was simply saving the city money. With the money he saved, he rebuilt Tampa's tattered roads, sewers, and neighborhoods. He also cut property taxes by over 50 percent. Because of Martínez's pro-business attitude, real estate developers streamed into Tampa. A boom in construction modernized the city's skyline.

Becomes Republican Governor of Florida

Martínez's success as mayor of Tampa convinced him to run for the governorship of Florida in 1986. Although he was elected, his term as governor was mired in problems. At the time, Florida had a reputation as the world capital of drug smuggling. Martínez tried to crack down on smugglers by calling for help from the National Guard. He also convinced the Florida legislature to pass stricter drug laws. In 1987 President Ronald Reagan appointed Martínez to the White House Conference on a Drug-Free America (originally a Democrat, he had switched to the Republican party in 1983).

However, Martínez quickly came under fire for his policies. He was criticized for building more prisons instead of developing programs to help drug addicts fight their habit so they might return to society as functioning members. Martínez also received criticism when he attempted to raise taxes and pass highly restrictive abortion laws. The Florida legislature defeated his efforts on both accounts.

"Martinez's term has been marked by political clumsiness," Gail DeGeorge remarked in *Business Week* at the time, "but his handling of abortion was in a class by itself." Martínez was politically hurt even further when he had members of the rap group 2 Live Crew arrested during a performance in Florida in 1990. He claimed that the group violated the state's obscenity law against offensive, indecent behavior. The arrests turned into a racial matter when minority groups accused the governor of enforcing the law only against black performers. In the ensuing court trial, the members of 2 Live Crew were found innocent of the charges against them. In the 1990 election for governor, Martínez was defeated.

Criticized as Nation's "Drug Czar"

Although he lost the state election, Martínez managed to find another position of authority. His friendship with then-U.S. President George Bush led to his appointment as director of the Office for National Drug Control Policy (ONDCP) in 1991. Created by Congress in 1989, the ONDCP is supposed to coordinate the war on drugs on both the state and federal levels. The ONDCP has to work closely with the Federal Bureau of Investigation, the Drug Enforcement Agency, and the Treasury Department. Overseeing the functioning of the ONDCP is the director, sometimes referred to as the "drug czar."

From the beginning, Martínez was criticized for his handling of the ONDCP. Critics charged that he staffed the organization with people who had little experience either in anti-drug work or in politics. Others felt that Martínez's laid-back management style did nothing to step up the war on drugs. Gordon White, writing in *U.S. News & World Report,* quoted a former Justice Department official who called Martínez a "colossal disappointment."

When Democrat Bill Clinton took over the presidency in 1992, he kept Martínez on as the director of the ONDCP, but cut the organization's staff from 146 to 25 employees.

For Further Information

Business Week, October 12, 1987; October 30, 1989.
Miami Herald, August 27, 1986; November 2, 1986.
New Republic, March 1, 1993, p. 8.
U.S. News & World Report, February 10, 1992, p. 33.
Guitar World, September 1986; February 1989.
Hispanic, March 1994, p. 48.
Musician, April 1987.
Time, November 26, 1990, pp. 88-89.

Eduardo Mata

Conductor
Born September 5, 1942, Mexico City, Mexico
Died January 4, 1995

"Classical music, like great painting, like all the arts and humanities ... belongs to everybody."

One of Mexico's most outstanding symphonic conductors, Eduardo Mata dedicated his entire life to music and has gained international recognition in the process. For 16 years he was music director of the Dallas Symphony Orchestra (DSO) in Texas, and he was credited with bringing the music of Hispanic composers to the rest of the world through his recordings with the symphony. Mata traveled widely, conducting orchestras from Japan to Australia to Germany. Throughout his career, he explored the works of such diverse composers as nineteenth-century French experimentalist Claude Debussy and twentieth-century American Aaron Copland.

Mata was born in Mexico City, Mexico, in 1942. Although his parents were not musicians, the family home was filled with the sounds of classical music. Mata learned to play the guitar as a child, but his real dream was to become a conductor. At the age of 11, he entered the National Conservatory of Mexico in Mexico City to study composition, piano, and conducting. When he was 18, he studied privately for four years with Mexican composer Carlos Chávez. He also received advanced training in conducting at the Tanglewood School, a renowned musical institute in Massachusetts.

In 1964, when he was only 22 years old, Mata was named musical director of the Guadalajara Symphony Orchestra in Mexico. Two years later he helped organize the Orquestra Filarmonia of the National University of Mexico City. He remained the ensemble's music director and conductor for the next ten years. During this time, he received invitations to conduct South American orchestras and smaller orchestras in the United States. By 1973 Mata had also become principal conductor of the Phoenix Symphony Orchestra in Arizona. The following year he made his London

Eduardo Mata

debut, conducting a performance by the London Symphony. He then accepted the position of music director with the Dallas Symphony Orchestra (DSO) in 1977.

Rebuilds Struggling Dallas Symphony

"I aim to give the Dallas Symphony a much more European sound than it has now," Mata told Sue Regan in *Gramophone* in 1978. He explained that "the typical sound of an American orchestra is more aggressive, more edgy and direct" than that of orchestras in Europe. But before he could change the sound of the Dallas Symphony, Mata had to reverse its dismal financial situation. When he took over the DSO, it was struggling back from bankruptcy. He set out to strengthen the ensemble by adding top-notch musicians. Knowing that a recording contract would increase the value of the DSO, he negotiated a deal with RCA Records. Dallas citizens began to take pride in the orchestra, and within ten years the DSO's audiences increased fourfold.

Mata's reputation spread across the United States and throughout the world. He served as a guest conductor with notable American orchestras in Atlanta, Boston, Chicago, Cleveland, Detroit, and San Francisco. In 1989 he became the principal guest conductor with the Pittsburgh Symphony. He also performed with symphony orchestras in Rotterdam (the Netherlands), Stuttgart (Germany), and Stockholm (Sweden).

Despite Mata's international travels, he did not forget the music of his homeland. "The great Hispanic composers [were] staples of his repertoire," Matthew Sigman observed in *Symphony,* "and he [brought] them to Dallas with great fervor." Mata realized, however, that bringing the music of these composers to the concert hall would not be enough. He knew that many people in the Hispanic communities of Texas could not afford the cost of symphony tickets. To reach them, he scheduled free outdoor concerts with the DSO. After Dallas's new Meyerson Symphony Center was built in 1989, Mata organized frequent open houses to encourage a more diverse audience to experience the magic of the symphony.

Brings Hispanic Music to the World

In 1985 Mata led the DSO on its first European tour, playing concerts in England, Germany, France, and Spain. In addition to a standard repertoire of American and European compositions, his recordings with the orchestra from this time showcase the works of Hispanic composers such as Antonio Estevez of Venezuela and Carlos Chávez,

who is considered by many music critics to be Mexico's leading composer of the twentieth century.

For his work in championing Hispanic music, Mata has received many awards. In Mexico he was honored with the Elías Sourasky Prize in the Arts, the Golden Lyre Award from the Mexican Union of Musicians, and lifetime membership in the prestigious Colegio Nacional—one of Mexico's highest honors. The president of Mexico awarded Mata the Mozart Medal in 1991. That same year, he was honored at the White House in Washington, D.C., with the Hispanic Heritage Award.

Recordings Offer Range of Composers

Mata conducted and recorded many pieces by European and American masters. His continued interest in presenting a broad and varied range of compositions stemmed from his firm belief in the universal nature of music: according to *Hispanic,* he once told a Dallas reporter that "classical music, like great painting, like all the arts and humanities ... belongs to everybody." During his years with the DSO, Mata performed works by famous European composers such as Maurice Ravel, Jean Sibelius, Peter Ilyich Tchaikovsky, and Sergey Rachmaninoff. In 1993 he and the DSO released an all-American program of works by Aaron Copland, Leonard Bernstein, and Roy Harris. "The musicmaking is something to cheer about," commented Richard Freed in *Stereo Review.*

In June of 1994 Mata retired from his position with the Dallas Symphony Orchestra. His 16-year tenure with the ensemble was one of the longest among present-day conductors. At the time of his retirement, Mata indicated he would still do free-lance work with other orchestras. As a certified pilot, he also planned to spend more time in the cockpit of his plane.Unfortunately, just six months later Mata was killed when the plane he was piloting crashed near Mexico City.

For Further Information

American Record Guide, March/April 1993, pp. 78-79.

Audio, April 1988, pp. 97-98.

Gramophone, May 1978, pp. 1841-42.

Hispanic, September 1991, pp. 41-43.

Stereo Review, January 1993, p. 96.

Symphony, November/December 1991, pp. 53-54.

Rachel McLish

Bodybuilder, actress
Born 1958, Harlingen, Texas

"If I was going to portray a Hispanic, it was going to be a Hispanic that I could relate to. Every Hispanic person that I know has something good going for them."

Rachel Livia Elizondo McLish is the woman who brought glamour to women's bodybuilding. Through her campaign against steroid abuse and her unique image as a "feminine bodybuilder," she became a role model for many women. She helped make weight-training and body shaping one of the fastest-growing exercise activi-ties for women in the 1980s. Although she still promotes physical fitness, she has turned her attention to acting, writing, and the fashion world.

McLish was born in 1958 in Harlingen, Texas, to Rafael and Rachel Elizondo. Her father, who came from a Spanish back-ground, was a neon sign-maker. Her mother, of Mexican-German heritage, was a home-maker. McLish's interest in fitness was first sparked by her study of ballet and by her father's weight-lifting hobby. Even as a child, she was fascinated by the strength and grace of the human body. The two very dif-ferent activities led her to believe that a woman with muscles could be both feminine and attractive.

During her high school years, Mclish found herself forced to choose between cheerleading and ballet. Even though she had dreamed since childhood of becoming a professional dancer, she opted for cheerlead-ing. It seemed to offer popularity and a full social life. By the time she enrolled at Pan American University in Texas, however, she regretted giving up her dream. At age 17, she believed she was already too old to pursue dancing again.

Misses Active Lifestyle

While studying at Pan American Univer-sity in Edinburg, Texas, McLish missed the physically active lifestyle she had known all her life. She decided to work with weights. At the time, weight-training wasn't very popular with the general public, and exercise clubs were scarce. McLish eventually found a place to work out called the "Shape Cen-ter." She loved the atmosphere there. Since her finances were already strained by college expenses, she couldn't afford the membership dues. McLish solved the problem by applying for a job teaching exercise classes at the center. She eventually became the center's manager.

In 1978 McLish earned her college degree in health and physical education and married her college sweetheart, John McLish. After the couple split up the following year, she formed a partnership with others to build the "Sport Palace," the first and largest health club facility in south Texas. The club was so successful it expanded to two other locations in Texas.

In 1980 McLish read about the first U.S. Women's Body Building Championship being held in Atlantic City. She was interested for two reasons: to promote her fitness centers, and to become a positive "feminine" example of a bodybuilder. She entered and won easily. Later that year she won the Ms. Olympia title—the highest award a female bodybuilder can receive.

As the first female bodybuilding champion, McLish was a new female role model. She appeared on magazine covers and television programs worldwide. She traveled and lectured on physiology (the study of the human body), diet, and beauty. Her dedication and effort paid off when she won the Ms. Olympia title again in 1982. She also won the World Championship that year.

Fights Against Steroid Use

By the mid-1980s, the emphasis in female bodybuilding shifted from muscle tone to massive muscular development. The use of steroid drugs for quick muscle growth became widespread. McLish stopped competing and campaigned against steroid and

Rachel McLish

other drug use. "My goal has always been systematic weight training to enhance my body—to build muscles to become more womanly and sensual," McLish related to Lisa Saenz in *Hispanic.* "Without steroids there is no way a woman can achieve [a significantly greater] degree of muscularity."

In 1984 McLish published *Flex Appeal,* a book on health, fitness, and nutrition (her second book on fitness, *Perfect Parts,* was published in 1987). Shortly after *Flex Appeal* appeared in bookstores, McLish became the spokesperson for the Health and Tennis Corporation of America. In 1990, McLish joined with K-Mart department stores to create a line of bodywear for active women. McLish took a hands-on approach to the fashion project and was actively involved in the construction of the garments. Her collection, "Rachel McLish for the Body Company," accounted for 28 percent of the total sales of athletic wear in the United States in 1991.

McLish's career in film began in 1985, when she had a starring role in *Pumping Iron II: The Women,* a documentary movie about the world of women's bodybuilding. She also starred in the 1991 CBS prime-time television special *Women of the 21st Century,* a documentary exploring women's commitment to a physical lifestyle.

Refuses Demeaning Roles in Films

When McLish first tried to pursue roles in feature films, she received offers to play "a female robojock, a female boxer, the typical roles you'd expect for a female bodybuilder," she explained to Saenz. She promptly turned them all down. She has also turned down roles that she finds demeaning to women or Hispanics. One such role was that of the character Vasquez in the 1986 hit *Aliens.* "Every other word was profane," McLish told Saenz, describing the role, "and if I was going to portray a Hispanic, it was going to be a Hispanic that I could relate to. Every Hispanic person that I know has something good going for them."

McLish's motion picture debut came in the 1992 film *Aces: Iron Eagle III,* which also featured Academy Award-winner Louis Gossett, Jr. In the film, McLish portrays Anna, a Peruvian woman who fights against a local drug lord who controls her hometown.

While continuing to pursue a film career, McLish also sets aside time to give speeches at high schools. She emphasizes the importance of education and urges students to attend college. In addition, she has set up scholarship funds for Hispanic students at Texas State Technical College in her hometown of Harlingen and at Pan American University, her alma mater.

For Further Information

Hispanic, September 1992, pp. 50-54.

McLish, Rachel, and Bill Reynolds, *Flex Appeal by Rachel,* Warner, 1984.

McLish, Rachel, and Joyce Vederal, *Perfect Parts,* Warner, 1987.

People, June 29, 1992, p. 68.

Nicholasa Mohr

Writer, artist
Born November 1, 1935, New York, New York

"Mohr continues to entertain readers of all ages and to challenge them to view the world with eyes open to new ideas and veiwpoints."

As a young girl, Nicholasa Mohr used her imagination to escape the poverty of her dismal neighborhood. As an adult, she uses this same creativity to express her feelings as a woman and as a Puerto Rican American. Mohr began her career as a fine arts painter and printmaker, then became a writer and illustrator of her own award-winning books.

Mohr was born in a barrio (a Spanish-speaking neighborhood) in New York City in 1935. Her parents, Pedro and Nicholasa Golpe, had migrated from Puerto Rico to America shortly after the beginning of the Great Depression in 1929. When she was eight years old, her father died. Poverty and prejudice constantly threatened to tear the family apart, and Mohr's mother struggled to keep it together. As the only girl of seven children, Mohr had to help her mother with the housework. Often stuck in her family's crowded apartment, she found freedom and adventure by drawing and painting.

Mohr's artistic talents brought her much praise in school. This in turn gave her extra confidence. Still, some of her classmates remained prejudiced against her because she was Hispanic. She was further humiliated when her high school counselor told her that, as a Puerto Rican girl, she should learn to sew rather than continue on with her education. Mohr refused to listen. After graduating high school in 1953, she managed to enroll in the Arts Students' League, an art school in New York. While studying there, she supported herself by working as a waitress, a factory worker, and a translator.

Mexico Inspires Art

At first, Mohr wanted to study art in Europe. After reading about the work of Mexican artists such as Diego Rivera (see **Diego Rivera**) and Jose Clemente Orozco, she decided instead to travel to Mexico City in 1956 to study their murals and paintings. The colors, figures, and methods of the Mexicans inspired her. She was especially drawn to the way those artists tried to bring about social change through their powerful artwork.

Mohr returned to the United States the following year and enrolled in the New School for Social Research where she met her future husband, psychologist Irwin Mohr. In 1959 she started taking classes at the Brooklyn Museum of Art School. She continued to work at her craft, developing her artistic style. Her life's experiences began to shape her work. Using bold letters and symbols, she told stories through her paintings.

Turns from Painting to Writing

This technique caught the eye of a publisher in New York. He tried to convince Mohr that she had the ability to become a writer. At first, she was reluctant to switch from painting to writing, but she soon wrote several short stories about growing up in a barrio. She was excited by the challenge of writing, a craft she found similar to painting. Writing allowed her the chance to draw pictures with words. After reading her stories, however, the publisher turned them down. Disappointed, Mohr returned to painting. A short while later, another publisher read her stories and offered her a book contract. Mohr then began work on her first novel.

Mohr's first book, *Nilda,* which contained eight of her own illustrations, was published in 1973. The novel traces the life of a young Puerto Rican girl, Nilda, growing up in Spanish Harlem (a New York City neighborhood) during World War II. She has to endure not only her family's poverty but prejudice from people outside her family. While the book focuses on the problems Nilda faces as she grows up, it also depicts her joys: spending time at summer camp,

Nicholasa Mohr

viewers applauded the stories for their realism and optimism. Like *Nilda, El Bronx Remembered* also received many awards, including being named a finalist for the prestigious National Book Award.

Two years later Mohr published another collection of short stories for young adults, *In Nueva York*. Mohr again focused on characters in Hispanic neighborhoods who had to confront poverty, racism, drugs, street gangs, and other problems. This time, however, she presented many of them in more than one story. Reviewers believed this gave readers a more intimate look into the lives of the characters, making them appear more real as they struggled to succeed. The American Library Association bestowed their Best Book Award in young adult literature on *In Nueva York*.

Explores the Character of Felita in Two Novels

Mohr wrote for a younger audience with the novel *Felita,* published in 1979. The book tells the story of a young Puerto Rican girl whose parents move to a nicer part of town, hoping to give their family a better life. Felita quickly misses her friends, and the rest of the family is soon discouraged by the discrimination they face there. After her family moves back to the old neighborhood, Felita still has problems with her classmates, but her grandmother helps her cope.

Mohr wrote about Felita once more in *Going Home,* which she published in 1986. In the novel, Felita is 11 years old, has a new boyfriend, and goes on vacation with her parents to Puerto Rico. Problems arise when her friends become jealous of her relationship with her boyfriend, and Felita becomes

finding a hidden garden, drawing. Many critics praised *Nilda* as a powerful yet sensitive story. Among the awards the book received was an outstanding book award in juvenile fiction from the *New York Times.*

In 1975 Mohr published *El Bronx Remembered,* a collection of short stories set in the Puerto Rican neighborhoods of New York City. The stories present the lives of many different characters—from a teenage Puerto Rican girl to an elderly Jewish man—and touch on the delicate subjects of death, incest, sexuality, and teen pregnancy. Re-

homesick while on vacation. By the end of the novel, however, she has learned to make new friends in Puerto Rico.

Mohr turned away briefly from fiction in 1993 when she published *All for the Better: A Story of El Barrio,* a biography of Evelina Lopez Antonetty. Because of the economic effects of the Great Depression, Lopez Antonetty had to move away from her family in Puerto Rico to live with an aunt in Spanish Harlem (El Barrio) in New York City in 1933. Over the years, she worked to improve not only her life but the lives of the people in the Hispanic community around her. She eventually founded the United Bronx Parents Group to work for solutions to the problems facing her community.

Although the majority of Mohr's writing has been directed at teenagers, she has stated in interviews that she doesn't write for them alone. She feels the characters and ideas in her works can appeal to people in all age groups. Mohr has no plans to change from writing to another art form. She believes writing has given her a chance both to express herself creatively and to address social issues that are important to her ethnic community. Mohr continues to entertain readers of all ages and to challenge them to view the world with eyes open to new ideas and viewpoints.

For Further Information

Authors and Artists for Young Adults, Volume 8, Gale Research, 1992, pp. 161-67.

Blicksilver, Edith, "Nicolasa Mohr," *Biographical Directory of Hispanic Literature in the United States,* edited by Nicolás Kanellos, Greenwood Press, 1989, pp. 199-213.

Hispanic Writers, Gale Research, 1991, pp. 314-15.

School Library Journal, May 1993, p. 118.

Pat Mora

Poet, writer
Born January 19, 1942, El Paso, Texas

"I take pride in being a Hispanic writer. I will continue to write and to struggle to say what no other writer can say in quite the same way."

When she was young and growing up in El Paso, Texas, Pat Mora was ashamed of her Mexican American heritage. In school she tried to look and act "American." At home she spoke Spanish only to her grandmother and her aunt, and she hated the Mexican music her father played on the radio. As she grew older, however, Mora realized she was denying a part of her identity, an essential part of who she was. She decided to accept herself fully and to share that acceptance with other Hispanics through her writings. "I take pride in being a Hispanic writer," she wrote in *Horn Book.* "I will continue to write and to struggle to say what no other writer can say in quite the same way."

Mora was born in El Paso in 1942 to Raul Antonio Mora and Estella Delgado. Her father worked as an optician while her mother cared for the family at home. The city of El Paso sits on the U.S. border with Mexico, across the Rio Grande River from the Mexican city of Juarez. The influence of Mexican culture in her hometown was strong, and Mora desperately tried to escape it while she was growing up.

After graduating from high school, Mora attended Texas Western College, earning her bachelor's degree in 1963. That same year she married William H. Burnside; the couple had three children before divorcing in 1981. During the mid-1960s, Mora taught in the El Paso Independent School District. In 1967 she earned her master's degree from the University of Texas at El Paso (UTEP), and within four years she was teaching English and communications part-time at El Paso Community College.

Learns the Value of Her Heritage

The early 1980s were important years in Mora's life. In 1981 she became the assistant to the vice president of academic affairs at UTEP. Around the same time, she finally realized that she could no longer deny her Mexican American heritage. This acceptance gave her a different outlook on life. She commented on her new approach in the *Christian Science Monitor:* "I revel in a certain Mexican passion not for life or about life, but *in* life, a certain intensity in the daily living of it."

Mora began writing poetry to express her new and intense feelings. Her desire to write, however, was not for herself alone. She felt American literature was missing the voices of Hispanic writers, and she wanted to help preserve her culture in that literature. "We need to be published and to be studied in schools and colleges," she wrote in *Horn Book,* "so that the stories and ideas of our people won't quietly disappear."

The quality of Mora's poetry was recognized quickly. In 1983 she won the Creative Writing Award from the National Association of Chicano Studies. The next year brought both personal and professional triumph for Mora. In addition to marrying her second husband, archaeologist Vernon Lee Scarborough, her first poetry collection, *Chants,* was published by the Arte Público Press of the University of Houston. The volume surveys the desert landscape within which Mora grew up. In many of the finely crafted poems, Mora depicts the desert as a woman; other times she presents women as the embodiment of the desert's strength. *Chants* received the Southwest Book Award, given by the Border Regional Library Association to outstanding works of literature about the Southwest.

In 1986 Arte Público published Mora's second book of verse, *Borders.* It, too, won the Southwest Book Award. The poetry in this collection explores all types of borders—including those between the United States and Mexico, and those between women and men. Many of the poems draw their inspiration from Mexican folk customs and the wisdom of native healers.

Hailed as a Poet and an Educator

While Mora was gaining fame as a poet, she was also getting recognition for her work as an educator. In 1987 she received the Chicano/Hispanic Faculty and Professional Staff Association Award for helping Hispanic students advance at UTEP. The following year she became director of the university's museum, as well as the assistant to the university's president.

In the autumn of 1989, Mora left the desert environment of El Paso and moved to the midwestern pastures of Ohio. At first, the loss of her Mexican American surroundings was unsettling to her. In an article she wrote for the *Christian Science Monitor,* Mora related that whenever she heard someone speaking Spanish in the Midwest, she automatically focused on the speaker: "I listen, silently wishing to be part of that other conversation—if only for a few moments, to feel Spanish in my mouth."

However, Mora quickly adapted to her new environment and expanded her artistic vision in the process. As she explained to Norma Alarcón in *Nuestro,* poetry taught her to use her "senses more keenly." In her third book of poetry, *Communion,* she examines larger themes, such as the way she relates to other women around her—and also to other people around the world.

Work Becomes Important Part of American Literature

Mora's desire to have the works of Hispanic writers included in the mainstream of American literature was finally realized in 1992. Harcourt Brace Jovanovich, the nation's largest textbook publisher, issued a high school English textbook titled *Mexican American Literature.* The 700-page book covers the works of Hispanic writers from colonial times to the present. Mora's work is included. Her poems are also featured in *The Norton Anthology of American Literature,* another highly respected textbook.

In the early 1990s Mora took on writing projects outside of poetry. In 1992 she published a children's book, *A Birthday Basket for Tia,* and the next year she published a book of essays, *Nepantla: Essays from the Land in the Middle.* These autobiographical essays describe her childhood in the desert

Pat Mora

around El Paso and how she has grown as a poet.

Mora believes her mission is to uphold her cultural identity, both for herself and for younger generations of Hispanic people. The best way she can do that, she explained in *Horn Book,* is through her gift of writing: "I want to give to others what writers have given me, a chance to hear the voices of people I will never meet."

For Further Information

Christian Science Monitor, July 18, 1990, pp. 16-17.
Hispanic Writers, Gale, 1991.
Horn Book, July/August 1990, pp. 436-37.
Nation, June 7, 1993, pp. 772-74.
Nuestro, March 1987, pp. 25-27.

Rita Moreno

Actress, singer, dancer
Born December 11, 1931, Humacao, Puerto Rico

"I have crossed over, but never, not for one minute, have I forgotten where I came from, or who I am. I have always been very proud to carry the badge of honor as a Hispanic."

Rita Moreno has brightened movie screens and theater stages with her talent since she was a teenager. In the beginning, she often had to accept stereotypical, ethnic roles in order to make a living, but she knew she was capable of more challenging parts. When she finally won an Academy award in 1962 for her portrayal of the character of Anita in *West Side Story,* she became one of the few Hispanics who was recognized as an international star. Since that time, she has won a Tony award, a Grammy award, and two Emmy awards, making her the only woman in the world to have received show business's four most prestigious honors.

Moreno was born Rosa Dolores Alverio in 1931 in the small town of Humacao, Puerto Rico. Her parents, Paco Alverio and Rosa María Marcano Alverio, divorced soon after her birth. Her mother left her with relatives in Puerto Rico and went to New York City to work as a seamstress. When Moreno was five years old, her mother returned for her. Along with other family members, Moreno traveled with her mother to live in New York City.

Moreno began dance lessons around this time, and attended New York Public School 132. She soon began performing in the children's theater at Macy's Department Store, at weddings, and at bar mitzvahs (the ceremony at which a Jewish boy, aged 13, attains the age of religious duty and responsibility). By the time she was 13, she had dropped out of school to pursue the life of an actress. She performed in nightclubs in New York, Boston, and Las Vegas. She also gained work in film, dubbing in Spanish for such actresses as Elizabeth Taylor and Margaret O'Brien.

Frustrated by Stereotypical Roles

Moreno's role in her first film, *So Young, So Bad* (1950), caught the eye of Hollywood mogul Louis B. Mayer. He immediately offered her a contract with his studio, Metro-Goldwyn-Mayer. Under the names Rosita Moreno (her stepfather's surname) and, later, Rita Moreno, she found parts in some twenty-five films during the 1950s, playing mostly ethnic roles. She became known as "Rita the Cheetah" because of the spicy parts she played and because of her highly publicized romances in real life. She was disheartened not only by the unfair nickname but also by the weak, stereotypical parts she was forced to play. She worked very hard to shed both.

Moreno's first satisfying acting role came in 1956. That year she played a slave girl in the hit musical *The King and I,* which starred Deborah Kerr and Yul Brynner. In the film Moreno had several scenes in which she acted well and sang beautifully. Despite this professional success, however, her career stalled in the late 1950s. She made few movies between 1956 and 1960. She returned to performing on the theater stage and was received well by critics. But she could not handle the mounting frustrations over her career—she attempted suicide with sleeping pills. When she awoke in a hospital, however, she realized that she wanted to live and went on to recovery.

Finds Success through West Side Story

In 1961 Moreno landed her most famous role: Anita in *West Side Story*. Loosely based on William Shakespeare's play *Romeo and Juliet,* the musical follows two rival gangs in New York—the Sharks (Hispanics) and the Jets (Anglos)—as they fight for turf. Two characters in the musical, Tony and Maria, fight to maintain their love in the face of their ethnic differences. Moreno lit up the screen with her singing, dancing, and convincing acting in *West Side Story*. The musical was an instant success. It won ten Academy awards, one of which was Moreno's for best supporting actress.

Moreno's performance in *West Side Story* propelled her to international stardom, and she began to receive roles over the next decade that were not based on her ethnicity. Even though she became a mainstream actress, she did not forget her roots. "I have crossed over, but never, not for one minute, have I forgotten where I came from, or who I am," she explained to Javier Bustillos and Anthony Chase in *Hispanic*. "I have always been very proud to carry the badge of honor as a Hispanic."

In 1965 Moreno met and married Dr. Leonard Gordon, a cardiologist. Their successful marriage has lasted to this day. In 1971 Moreno began to work in television. She appeared on *The Electric Company,* a

Rita Moreno

television series for older children. For her participation in the show's soundtrack recording, she won a Grammy award for the best recording for children in 1972.

Pokes Fun at Stereotypes

In 1975 Moreno was a hit in the Broadway play, *The Ritz.* She portrayed her character—a Puerto Rican singer named Googie Gómez—in an outrageously comic manner to point fun at all the stereotypes she had played over the years. Some worried that her performance would offend Hispanics, but Moreno thought otherwise. "The Spanish people who come backstage say they love what I'm doing," she told a reporter for the *New York Times*. "Of course, some *Latins* might take offense, but I don't want to meet them. I don't want to talk to anyone who doesn't have a sense of humor about themselves." For her portrayal of Googie, Moreno won a Tony award in 1975 for best supporting actress in a play.

Displaying her trademark versatility, Moreno returned to television and won an Emmy award in 1977 for her guest appearances on *The Muppet Show.* She won another Emmy the following year for her appearance on an episode of the detective show *The Rockford Files.* In the later 1970s, she developed a nightclub song-and-dance act that she performed on cruise ships and in cities across the country.

Throughout the 1980s, Moreno continued her acting work, especially on the stage. Despite her hectic schedule, she made time to promote Hispanic causes and to appear before Hispanic groups. As she explained to Bustillos and Chase, she and her husband "are very involved in trying to make the Hispanic community understand that education is everything." For her positive portrayal of Hispanics on film and in the theater, Moreno was named one of ten Hispanic Women of the Year by *Hispanic* magazine in 1989. The following year she was awarded the White House Hispanic Heritage Award.

Moreno continues to expand her career as a star of stage, screen, and television with roles that reflect her many talents. In the fall of 1994, Hispanic actors began to play more key roles on high-profile television series. Moreno was among them, landing a major role on the NBC television series *The Cosby Mysteries,* starring Bill Cosby.

For Further Information

Hispanic, October 1989, pp. 30-33; September 1990, p. S6.
Ms. January/February 1991, pp. 93-95.
New York Times, March 1975.
Suntree, Susan, *Rita Moreno,* Chelsea House, 1992.

Joaquín Murieta

Folk hero, bandit
Born c. 1830, Sonora, Mexico
Died July 1853, California

"The facts surrounding the life and times of Joaquín Murieta are few, but the legends, tall tales, and rumors are many."

Following the gold rush fever of 1848, the hills of California were filled with luckless gold diggers turned bandits. Stories of the notorious antics and eventual death of one, Joaquín Murieta (sometimes spelled "Murrieta"), grew into a folk tale. This was due mainly to the 1854 publication of John Rollin Ridge's book, *The Life and Adventures of Joaquín Murieta, the Celebrated California Bandit.* In 1881 the novel was published in serial form by the Santa Barbara newspaper *La gaceta,* lending some substance to the myth. The facts surrounding the life and times of Joaquín Murieta are few, but the legends, tall tales, and rumors are many.

Born in the Mexican state of Sonora around 1830, Murieta reportedly came to California in search of farmland and a better life. When gold was discovered, he quickly gave up farming for mining. For reasons lost to history, bad-hearted Americans abused Murieta's family. His wife was assaulted, his brother was hanged, and he was beaten. Murieta retaliated in the only way he knew how—by becoming a horse thief in 1851. He reportedly committed his crimes in the name of ethnic honor and revenge, which gained him some sympathy and fame among Californians.

Hunted by Rangers

Murieta and his band of outlaws repeatedly terrorized the California countryside with murders and robberies. Local authorities posted a $1,000 reward for his capture. At least one member of his group had also achieved notoriety—an unfortunate accident led Jack García to be known as Three-Fingered Jack. In the spring of 1853, the California legislature hired a group of rangers to track down Murieta and put an end to his misdeeds. Led by Captain Harry Love, a Mexican-American War veteran, the group was given three months to stop the crime wave.

A few days before the deadline, Love and his rangers surprised a band of Mexican horsemen near Tulare Lake in south-central California. The rangers insisted that one of the horsemen was Murieta. Furious gunplay followed and the Mexicans were killed. To prove their success and claim their reward, the rangers cut off Murieta's head and García's three-fingered hand and preserved them in alcohol. The morbid souvenirs were later placed on exhibit by the businesslike Captain Love.

From the very beginning, there has been some doubt that the infamous head actually belonged to Murieta. This led to more speculation on his whereabouts and his further adventures. Murieta's legend began in 1854 with the publication of Ridge's book, which romanticized the bandit's supposed deeds. Over the years, his legend grew as it was rewritten and expanded on in subsequent books, poems, and ballads. Much later, Hollywood used the stories passed down about Murieta as a basis for the colorful but more law-abiding characters of the Cisco Kid and Zorro.

For Further Information

Latta, Frank Forrest, *Joaquín Murrieta and His Horse Gangs,* Bear State Books, 1980.

Neruda, Pablo, *Splendor and Death of Joaquín Murieta,* Farrar, Straus, and Giroux, 1972.

Ridge, John Rollin, *The Life and Adventures of Joaquín Murieta, the Celebrated California Bandit,* University of Oklahoma Press, 1955.

Sports Afield, July 1989, pp. 81, 97-98.

Antonia Novello

Former surgeon general of the United States
Born August 23, 1944, Fajardo, Puerto Rico

"I hope that being the first woman and minority surgeon general ... enables me to reach many individuals with my message of empowerment for women, children, and minorities."

Antonia Novello was the first female and first Hispanic to be appointed surgeon general of the United States. As a former pediatrician, her focus was on the health concerns of children and youth. As leader of the 6,500 employees of the Public Health Service, she directed the nation's attention to

Antonia Novello

AIDS-infected children, the perils of smoking and teenage drinking, and women's health issues.

Antonia Coello Novello as born in 1944 in Fajardo, Puerto Rico, to Antonio Coello and Ana Delia Coello. When she was eight years old, her father died, and she and her brothers were raised by their mother, a school teacher. As a child, Novello suffered from a painful chronic illness of the colon (a section of the large intestine). She was hospitalized every summer for treatments for the disease, and learned what it is like to be a helpless patient. Her condition was finally corrected by surgery when she was 18 years old. These experiences convinced her to pursue a career in medicine. She wanted to help other children who were suffering as she had.

Novello earned her bachelor of science degree from the University of Puerto Rico in 1965. She continued her studies at the university, earning her medical doctor (M.D.) degree in 1970. That same year she married Joseph Novello, a U.S. Navy flight surgeon. The two then moved to Ann Arbor, Michigan, to continue their medical training at the University of Michigan Medical Center. Novello worked in the pediatric nephrology unit, treating children with kidney diseases. For her skilled and caring treatment of patients, Novello was honored with the Intern of the Year award by the center's pediatrics (children's health) department. She was the first woman to have received the award.

Novello continued her medical training at Georgetown University in Washington, D.C. In 1982 she earned a master's degree in public health from Johns Hopkins University in Baltimore, Maryland. In 1986 she became deputy director of the National Institute of Child Health and Human Development. In this position, she took a special interest in children with AIDS (Acquired Immune Deficiency Syndrome). At the same time, Novello served as a professor of pediatrics at Georgetown University Hospital.

Noticed by the president

Novello earned a reputation in the medical field and in Washington as a cooperative, dedicated, and quiet physician. In the early 1980s, she had served on a Congressional staff, giving advice to lawmakers on such medical issues as organ transplants and cigarette warning labels. President George Bush, elected in 1988, was impressed by her ideas on many medical-legal issues. In the fall of

1989 he nominated Novello to be the country's next surgeon general.

The role of surgeon general—the symbolic doctor for all Americans—is a public one. Instead of seeing individual patients, the surgeon general tries to inform the public about problems or trends in medicine. The surgeon general is also head of the United States Public Health Service. This organization, associated with the U.S. Navy, is composed of medical professionals who hold military rank. They serve on Native American reservations and in other areas of the country where there is a shortage of doctors. In her position, Novello held the rank of Vice Admiral and wore a military uniform trimmed with gold braid.

Each month, the surgeon general receives several hundred invitations to speak about medical issues. The opportunity to influence people on health matters is great. Shortly after her appointment, Novello visited her birthplace in Puerto Rico. "When I got off the plane, kids from my mother's school lined both sides of the road handing me flowers," Novello related to a reporter for the *Washington Post.* "I went to the [veterans] hospital to speak. When the veterans saw my gold braid they all stood and saluted.... I realized that for these people, for women, I have to be good as a doctor, I have to be good as a surgeon general, I have to be everything."

During her term as surgeon general, Novello attempted to solve many problems. Concerned about the dangers of teenage drinking, she met with some of the largest beer and wine companies in the country and asked them to stop aiming their advertising at young people. She criticized the tobacco industry and lectured the public on the dangers of smoking. She was particularly disturbed by rising lung cancer rates among females. During her hectic schedule, she found time to visit many hospitals to give hugs and encouragement to children and AIDS victims.

AIDS and its long-term effect on children was an especially important issue for Novello. "AIDS is the only epidemic in the world where children will survive their parents," she told Carol Krucoff in the *Saturday Evening Post.* "By the year 2000, we might have as many as 10 million children who are orphans of this epidemic. We've got to do the best we can for all children."

When she was chosen to be surgeon general, Novello told Tonya E. Wolford of *Hispanic,* "I hope that being the first woman and minority surgeon general ... enables me to reach many individuals with my message of empowerment for women, children, and minorities." When her term finally ended in 1993, many people believed she had done just that.

For Further Information

Hawxhurst, Joan C., *Antonia Novello: U.S. Surgeon General,* Millbrook Press, 1993.

Hispanic, January/February 1990, p. 20; October 1991, p. 15.

People, December 17, 1990, pp. 109-110.

Saturday Evening Post, May/June 1991, pp. 38-41, 93.

Washington Post, October 18, 1989; October 24, 1989; May 8, 1990.

Ellen Ochoa

Astronaut
Born May 10, 1958, Los Angeles, California

"If you stay in school, you have the potential to achieve what you want in the future."

As a little girl in California, Ellen Ochoa wasn't sure what she wanted to be when she grew up. Even in college, she changed her major five times. She went from music to business to journalism to computer science, before finally settling on physics. Her career choice proved to be the right one. Before the age of 33, she had received three patents in optical processing (patents are documents issued by the government legally recognizing the creation of an invention or product). The year she turned 33, she become America's first female Hispanic astronaut.

Ochoa was born in 1958 in Los Angeles, California, to Rosanne Deardorff and Joseph Ochoa. Her father, a native Californian, was of Mexican descent. Her parents divorced when she was in junior high school. Ochoa, her sister, and her three brothers were then raised by their mother in La Mesa, California. Ochoa's mother instilled the value of education in all her children at an early age.

Ochoa took her mother's advice to heart. She was always an excellent student, but she did exceptionally well in math and science. When she was 13, she won the San Diego County spelling bee. In junior high school she was named outstanding seventh and eighth grade girl. Consistently at the head of her class, Ochoa graduated as valedictorian from her high school in La Mesa. She repeated that feat at San Diego State University where she earned her bachelor of science degree in physics in 1980.

While in school, Ochoa also won honors for her musical ability. She was named her high school's top musician. In 1983 she was a student soloist winner with the Stanford Symphony Orchestra. With her many achievements in the field of music, she considered playing the flute for a career, but decided science would be a more stable field. She continues playing the flute as a hobby.

Research Developments Earn Patents

Ochoa continued her education at Stanford University in California. She earned a master's degree in electrical engineering in 1981 and a doctorate degree in that field in 1985. Following her graduate studies, she became a research engineer at Sandia National Laboratories in Livermore, California. Scientists, inventors, and artists sometimes struggle all their lives to develop ideas or inventions that they can patent and claim as their own. Ochoa's three patents for processes she developed in the field of optics (the study of light and vision) came within a few years after she had begun working at the laboratory.

It was a combination of Ochoa's many talents that won her a job with the National Aeronautics and Space Administration (NASA). She had first applied to the astronaut program in 1985. Two years later she was named one of the top 100 finalists. She began her work at NASA as a researcher, then became a supervisor over 40 other scientists.

Ellen Ochoa

In 1989 she received the Hispanic Engineer Achievement Award for the most promising engineer in government. The following year she became one of 23 new astronauts chosen by NASA for the Space Shuttle program. She reached another milestone in her life in 1990 by marrying Coe Fulmer Miles.

Ochoa takes her status as a role model for young Hispanics very seriously. Since her selection as an astronaut, she has often spoken to Hispanic students and community groups. Her message to them is simple: "If you stay in school you have the potential to achieve what you want in the future," she told Kim Bergheim in *Hispanic*. "Education increases career options and gives you a chance for a wide variety of jobs."

Space Musician and Scientist

In 1993 Ochoa became the first Hispanic female to travel in space. On the space shuttle Discovery, she and other crew members undertook the ATLAS 2 mission. ATLAS stands for Atmospheric Laboratory for Applications and Science. During her nine days in space, she orbited the earth 148 times.

While in orbit, Ochoa became the first astronaut to play a flute in space. She entertained her crewmates with military and national anthems and some classical music. She also held a space-to-ground ham radio conversation with students in her hometown of La Mesa, California. She told them what it felt like to float in space and explained the primary goal of the ATLAS 2 mission, which was to study the earth's atmosphere. The astronauts on the mission were particularly concerned with studying the ozone layer (an atmospheric layer at heights of approximately 20 to 30 miles that protects the earth

from harmful solar radiation and has been diminished over past several decades by a variety of manmade causes, including automobile exhaust) to find any depletion in it.

Ochoa's most important job during the mission, however, was to operate the shuttle's 50-foot robot arm to send a 2,800-pound satellite into space. The satellite was programmed to gather information about solar wind and the sun's corona (the outermost part of the atmosphere of the sun). The world watched as Ochoa captured the satellite a day later and returned it to the cargo bay so scientists on Earth could study the data it collected.

Ochoa hopes to revisit space when her turn comes up next. In the astronaut rotation, that could mean a wait of a year or two. In the meantime, she continues her work with NASA and visits schools to encourage students to stay focused on their goals.

For Further Information

Hispanic, May 1990, pp. 18-19.
Notable Hispanic American Women, Gale Research, 1993, pp. 296-99.
San Diego Union-Tribune, May 12, 1993, p. A1.

Edward James Olmos

Actor
Born February 24, 1947, Los Angeles, California

"I come from a dysfunctional family, I'm a minority, I have no natural talent, but I did it. If I can do it, anybody can do it. I take away all the excuses."

Edward James Olmos is an actor with a very active social conscience. He has created memorable characters on television, in plays, and in movies. But his greatest enjoyment comes from influencing young people to do something good with their lives. Each year Olmos makes time to give more than one hundred speeches to groups of disadvantaged kids. He encourages them to get an education and to take control of their own destinies.

Olmos's passion for education is a gift from his parents. He was born in 1947 in East Lost Angeles, California, to Pedro Olmos and Eleanor Huizar. His father had left Mexico City, Mexico, at the age of 21 with nothing more than a sixth-grade education. After settling in Los Angeles, his father returned to school and eventually earned a high school degree. Olmos's mother left school after the eighth grade, but she, too, returned to school to complete her education after the children were grown.

Olmos's parents divorced when he was eight years old. It was a traumatic time for him, and he responded by concentrating on baseball. He explained that baseball was the only thing that made him stop thinking about his own problems. He practiced the sport every day, and he won the Golden State (California) batting championship while he was still a schoolboy. Through his concentration on baseball, he developed a tremendous sense of self-discipline that has remained with him as an adult.

Baseball to Music to Acting

Olmos's father was certain that his son would become a professional ball player. At the age of 15, however, Olmos suddenly changed his goals. Instead of becoming a ball player, he decided he would be a singer and dancer. By the time he graduated from high school, he was earning money as the leader of a band called Pacific Ocean. The group played regularly at top nightclubs in Los Angeles.

"I sang terrible," Olmos told *New York*'s Pete Hamill, "but I could scream real good and I could dance. So I'd dance for five minutes, then come back and sing a couple more screams, then dance again."

During the day, Olmos attended East Los Angeles College. At night, he brought his books along on Pacific Ocean's jobs and studied during breaks. He eventually earned an associate's degree in sociology. Hoping to improve his singing, Olmos returned to the college to take a drama course. Before long, he fell in love with acting and decided to make it his career goal.

Starts Out as a "Bad Guy"

By the time he was 25, Olmos was married to Kaija Keels, and had two sons, Mico and Bodie. He supported his family by running an antique furniture delivery business. To satisfy his acting desires, he found work with experimental theater groups at night. At the same time, he also tried out for small roles on television. He frequently won bit parts on TV police shows, often playing the role of the "bad guy."

In 1978 Olmos won the role that changed his life as an actor. It was a part in *Zoot Suit,* a musical drama written by Luis Valdez (see **Luis Valdez**). The story was based on an actual 1942 case in which a group of Hispanic youths were wrongly convicted of murder in Los Angeles. Olmos played the

Edward James Olmos

Portrays Mexican Folk Hero

Olmos's next film, *The Ballad of Gregorio Cortez,* was deeply meaningful to him. It was the tale of a Mexican folk hero who traditionally had been portrayed as a fierce bandit. Through research, however, Olmos discovered that Cortez was actually a poor rancher and dedicated family man. He had became the subject of the largest manhunt in Texas history simply because of a misunderstood word. Olmos decided to portray Cortez as an ordinary man who was victimized because of discrimination and ignorance.

Olmos spoke Spanish in *The Ballad of Gregorio Cortez,* which carried no English subtitles (translation). Although the film appeared on public television, no major movie studio chose to distribute it. In response, Olmos rented a Hollywood theater and showed the film every Saturday morning for free. He traveled extensively to promote the film. During this period, he turned down film and television roles because he felt they would take up too much of his time. One of those roles was on the popular television series *Hill Street Blues.*

One television role Olmos eventually agreed to play was that of Lieutenant Martin Castillo on *Miami Vice.* This immensely popular series, which began its five-year run in 1985, made Olmos's face known nationwide. Although unhappy with the series as a whole (he thought its storylines were weak), Olmos found his character interesting. "He embodies concepts," Olmos explained to *Playboy*'s Marcia Seligson, "that I think are essential to getting to the highest level of understanding oneself— discipline, determination, perseverance, and patience." For his riveting performance on the series,

macho "El Pachuco," the narrator of the story. Strutting across the stage, Olmos delivered a powerful, attention-getting performance. *Zoot Suit* electrified Los Angeles and awakened the city to its Chicano (Mexican American) community. Scheduled for a tenday run, the play actually ran for a year and a half. It then moved to Broadway, where Olmos was nominated for a Tony award for his performance.

After *Zoot Suit* Olmos no longer had to fight for one-line parts on TV shows. He was offered feature roles in major films. Worried about becoming locked into stereotyped Hispanic roles, however, he selected his projects carefully. One of his memorable roles from this time was in the 1982 science fiction thriller *Blade Runner,* which starred Harrison Ford.

Olmos was honored with an Emmy award for best supporting actor in a dramatic series in 1985 and a Golden Globe award in 1986.

Dives into Role of Math Teacher

Olmos was more enthusiastic, however, about his role in the 1988 film *Stand and Deliver.* The movie presents the true story of Jaime Escalante (see **Jaime Escalante**), a Bolivian-born math teacher who came to a gang-filled Los Angeles high school. There, he inspired 18 students to take—and pass—an advanced placement calculus test. Along the way, Escalante also taught them to have pride in themselves and to take control of their own futures.

"The film is really about the triumph of the human spirit," Olmos told Seligson. "It's about something we've lost—the joy of learning, the joy of making our brains develop." To prepare for his role as Escalante, Olmos attended the teacher's classes, studied Escalante's mannerisms, and gained 40 pounds. For his realistic portrayal, Olmos received an Academy award nomination.

Next, Olmos directed and starred in *American Me,* a 1992 film about rising street crime in the Los Angeles barrio (Spanish-speaking neighborhood) where he grew up. *American Me* presented the brutal, realistic story of a gang member's life, in and out of prison. "The film is not for one race, one subculture, one age range," Olmos told Jack Kroll in *Newsweek.* "Gangs teach a distorted discipline, a distorted familial bonding, a distorted sense of pride and power."

Dedicated to Public Service

Throughout his career, Olmos has dedicated his time to public service work. He has helped to make peace among Los Angeles's warring gangs, has worked with disabled and sexually abused children, and has spoken out against drug abuse. After the 1992 Los Angeles riots resulting from the court decision in the Rodney King beating trial (in which four white police officers were acquitted of savagely beating King, a black man, despite graphic video-taped evidence of the assault), Olmos was one of the first people to appear on the streets of Los Angeles to begin the clean-up. He then met with local and state officials to develop plans for rebuilding. As a member of the Rebuild L. A. Committee, he was intimately involved in the process.

Olmos continues his social activities, often visiting children in juvenile halls, in inner-city schools, and on Native American reservations. He brings them the message that it is possible to improve one's lot in life, even against heavy odds. He is proof of that. "I come from a dysfunctional family, I'm a minority, I have no natural talent, but I did it," Olmos explained to Kroll. "If I can do it, anybody can do it. I take away all the excuses."

For Further Information

Hispanic, September 1988, pp. 29-33.
Newsweek, March 30, 1992, pp. 66-67.
New York, September 29, 1986.
Playboy, June 1989.
Washington Post, March 21, 1992, p. B1.

Sandra Ortiz-Del Valle

Basketball referee
Born April 23, 1951, New York, New York

"Many think I am into [being a basketball referee] for the novelty. The players and coaches who know me recognize that I am serious and respect me."

S andra Ortiz-Del Valle is a rarity—a woman who works in the world of men's professional sports. She has quietly broken down boundaries in the male-dominated sporting world by becoming one of the few women basketball referees working in the United States Basketball League. Her skills and discipline have earned her a spot in the Naismith Basketball Hall of Fame.

Ortiz-Del Valle was born in New York City in 1951 to Esteban and Delia Ortiz. Her father worked as an electrician, while her mother served as the only Hispanic on the local school board. From her Puerto Rican parents, Ortiz-Del Valle learned the importance of self-improvement and determination.

Sports Keep Her in Line

As a child, Ortiz-Del Valle turned to sports as a way to stay out of trouble. She got hooked on basketball while in high school. In 1974 she graduated from New York's City College with a bachelor of science degree in education. She earned her master's degree in administration and supervision from the college in 1983. It was while playing women's college basketball that Ortiz-Del Valle first started refereeing, beginning with youth games in 1978.

Ortiz-Del Valle quickly became attracted to a possible career as a referee. To increase her skills, she took courses. In 1984 she started working in semi-professional leagues. By 1989 her ability and reputation caught the attention of the USBL and they offered her a job.

The USBL is composed of some of the best basketball players in the United States. A number of players in the league could make it to the National Basketball Association (NBA). Ortiz-Del Valle's ultimate goal is to work as a referee in the NBA.

Still Faces Opposition

Even after a dozen years as a referee, Ortiz-Del Valle still finds that she must prove herself as a legitimate basketball official. She has met with some resistance in the male-dominated sport. "When I am faced with people new to the idea of a woman referee in a men's league, they think I have to pay my dues, and many think I am in it for the novelty," she explained to Robyn Kleerekoper in *Notable Hispanic American Women.* "The players and coaches who know me recognize that I am serious and respect me."

Ortiz-Del Valle is a member of the International Professional Basketball Officials Association. In addition to her basketball career, she is a full-time physical education teacher at Humanities High School in New York. She also coaches bowling and boys' baseball there. The media attention to her career as a referee has produced at least one positive effect: The girls at her school look up to her as a role model.

For Further Information

Notable Hispanic American Women, Gale, 1993, pp. 306-07.

Elizabeth Peña

Actress
Born September 23, 1959, Elizabeth, New Jersey

"I've never thought of [being Hispanic] as an obstacle. I think it's good. There are certainly enough five-foot-seven blonds."

Elizabeth Peña

Elizabeth Peña never considered her ethnic looks or heritage an obstacle to her goals. She was shocked in high school to lose the role of a midwestern farm girl in a school production because she just didn't look the part. Through determination and hard work combined with a gift for acting, Peña has proven herself a versatile and sought-after actress.

Peña was born in 1959 in Elizabeth, New Jersey (her parents named her after the town). She was the first daughter of actor, writer, and director Mario Peña and producer Estella Marguerita Toirac Peña. Four months after her birth, her parents took her back to their home country of Cuba. At the time, the Cuban Revolution was underway. Fidel Castro and others had overthrown Fulgencio Batista, the brutal dictator who had ruled Cuba throughout the 1950s. The Peñas believed Cuba would become a land of greater opportunity under Castro's government.

Unfortunately, Mario Peña was sent to a Cuban prison upon his return. Castro's Communist government disapproved of his poems and political views. When he was finally released, he had no choice but to leave the country and return to the United States. Peña, her mother, and her younger sister were not allowed to follow him until 1968.

Mother Opposes Career Choice

After being reunited, the family settled in New York City. Peña's parents founded the city's Latin American Theater Ensemble, and became respected and well-known figures in New York's theater community. The young Peña was inspired to pursue acting by her parents' example, even though her mother wished she would try a more stable career. Against her mother's wishes, Peña enrolled in New York's famous High School of Performing Arts. After she graduated from the school, she continued to study acting and clowning with various theater groups and private teachers.

Peña's determination eventually convinced her mother that she was in the right field. Beginning in 1979, it also earned her a number of small roles on the stage and in movies. In the theater, she played such roles as Juliet in *Romeo and Juliet* and Beba in *Night of the Assassins.* In movies, she played opposite actors such as James Caan in *Thief* (1981) and Rubén Blades (see **Rubén Blades**) in *Crossover Dreams* (1985).

Moves to Hollywood

Success in New York spurred Peña to move to Hollywood to search for larger roles. She wanted a role in *Down and Out in Beverly Hills,* a 1986 film starring Richard Dreyfuss and Bette Midler. She decided to flood the casting director's office with her pictures and messages. The ploy worked: Peña managed to earn a screen test and won the role of a maid in the film. Critics praised her sexy and funny portrayal, and her Hollywood career was launched.

1987 was a busy year for Peña. She won a role in *La Bamba,* the film biography of the late Mexican American singer Ritchie Valens (see **Ritchie Valens**). In the hit film, Peña played the part of the abused-yet-loyal wife of Ritchie Valens's older brother. That same year, she earned a role in the television series *I Married Dora.* However, the situation comedy, about a man who marries his Central American maid so she won't be

deported, was panned by critics. Peña then finished out the year with a role in a Steven Spielberg film, **batteries not included.*

In 1988 Peña took a break from acting to marry William Stephan Kibler, a movie agent turned junior high school teacher. That year she accepted a number of awards, including the Hispanic Women's Council Woman of the Year award, the New York Image award, the U.S. Congressional award, and the Nosotros Golden Eagle award.

Biggest Role Comes in Eerie Picture

Peña resumed her acting career in 1990. She landed her biggest role to date in the movie *Jacob's Ladder.* She played the part of Tim Robbins's mysterious girlfriend in the eerie picture about a Vietnam veteran struggling to hold onto reality. Her part was not originally written for a Hispanic actress, but Peña was able to convince the producers of the film to change it. Her persistence paid off once again. A reviewer for *Newsweek* magazine called her performance "warm and gritty."

That same year, Peña was cast as a client/secretary of a heartbroken lawyer in the television show *Shannon's Deal.* Critics treated the show unkindly, but gave Peña high marks for her work. The *Washington Post*'s Tom Shales, quoted in *People,* maintained that Peña was "assertive and gutsy.... Maybe the show should be about *her.*"

Although Peña has yet to be the star of a movie or successful television show, she is happy with her career and with the kinds of roles she has been offered. She does not expect to be limited to playing Hollywood stereotypes of Hispanic women. "I've never thought of [being Hispanic] as an obstacle," she explained to Tim Allis and Nancy Matsumoto in *People.* "I think it's good. There are certainly enough five-foot-seven blondes."

For Further Information

Contemporary Theater, Film, and Television, Volume 5, Gale Research, 1988.
Newsweek, November 12, 1990, pp. 77-78.
People, May 13, 1991, pp. 107-08.

Federico Peña

U.S. secretary of transportation, former mayor
of Denver
Born March 15, 1947, Laredo, Texas

Federico Peña

"It's taken me time to understand there will always be someone who opposes me. I have had to learn to be a little more thick-skinned, yet not become an insensitive armadillo."

As secretary of the U.S. Department of Transportation, Federico Peña is responsible for the smooth operation of the nation's highways, airports, and railroad networks. This job follows his earlier work as mayor of Denver, Colorado. While mayor for two terms, he revitalized the city through major construction projects, including the building of a new airport.

Federico Fabian Peña was born in 1947 into a Texas family whose ancestors had been politicians. His great grandfather had been mayor of Laredo, Texas, during the American Civil War. Peña was the third of six children born to Gustavo and Lucia Peña. Theirs was a strict family. While growing up, the Peña children addressed their parents as "sir" and "ma'am," and were punished for disrespect or swearing.

Peña and his brothers were altar boys at the Sacred Heart Catholic Church and attended St. Joseph's Academy high school. Standard achievement tests were not easy for Peña. He had to study long hours to earn good grades in school. Still, he managed to graduate with honors, and his classmates voted him "most likely to succeed." He attended the University of Texas at Austin where he was active in campus politics and took part in Vietnam War protests. After graduating with a bachelor's degree in 1969, he enrolled at the University of Texas Law School. He earned his law degree in 1972.

Moves to Denver and Enters Politics

Peña joined his brother Alfredo in Denver to form a law partnership, Peña and Peña. In addition, he worked for the Mexican American Legal Defense and Educational Fund (see **Antonia Hernández**), and for the Chicano Education Project. As the legal advisor for this last group, he pushed for better schools in Hispanic neighborhoods. Through his activities in the Hispanic community, he became interested in politics. In 1978 he made a successful run for the Colorado House of Representatives. Peña was so committed to his work in the House that his colleagues named him outstanding legislator of the year in 1981.

In 1983 Peña surprised political analysts by winning the election for mayor of Denver. He replaced the man who had held the job for 14 years. This was especially notable since the Hispanic population of the city was relatively small. But Peña had captured the interest of most of the voters with his campaign slogan, "Denver: Imagine a Great City." At age 36, he became one of the youngest mayors in the United States and the first Hispanic mayor of Denver.

Like many older American cities, Denver was suffering from a slow economy, air pollution, and inner-city decay. Peña had a tough job convincing businessmen, citizens, and politicians that drastic change was needed to save the city. During his first four-year term, he made little progress and was harshly criticized.

Barely Escapes Recall

"It's taken me time to understand there will always be someone who opposes me," Peña explained to Ann Carnahan in the *Rocky Mountain News.* "I have had to learn to be a little more thick-skinned, yet not become an insensitive armadillo." Peña had to fight hard to win re-election in 1987. A few months after his victory, he was almost ousted from office when citizens started a petition drive to recall him. The drive fell 2,000 signatures short.

Peña was finally able to convince diverse groups of citizens to cooperate with his plans during his second term in office, and Denver began to make an economic comeback. Peña arranged for the construction of the new $2.3 billion Denver International Airport—the largest airport in the world—and a convention center. He had city workers clean up neighborhoods, plant thousands of trees, and repair streets and bridges. He introduced pollution controls that dramatically improved the city's air. For his accomplishments, Peña received the City Livability award from the U.S. Conference of Mayors in 1990. In 1991 he received the American Planning Association's Distinguished Leadership award.

In 1988 Peña had married Ellen Hart, a lawyer and former English teacher. They have two daughters. To spend more time with his family and to seek new challenges in his life, Peña decided not to run for a third term as mayor of Denver in 1991.

Invited to Washington

In 1992 President Bill Clinton offered Peña the challenge he was seeking. Clinton invited Peña to become a member of his cabinet as the new head of the Department of Transportation. Peña's reputation as a successful mayor and his work as a member of Clinton's transition team on transportation issues helped earn him the job. In 1993 Peña took charge of the country's transportation systems and the 110,000 people who operate them.

One of the issues facing Peña when he assumed his post as secretary of transportation dealt with airlines. He was opposed to restrictions that foreign countries placed on American airlines. He felt those restrictions went against agreements America already had with those countries, and he worked to remove them.

One of Peña's top priorities inside the country has been highway safety. He is concerned about the numbers of citizens who are injured or lose their lives in auto accidents every year and the resulting costs to government and taxpayers. He notes that teenagers are especially at risk.

"I think most young people in the country don't realize that, between the ages of 5 and 34 years of age, the leading cause of death in our country is on our highways," Peña explained in an interview with Lark McCarthy that was broadcast on *Fox Morning News* on December 15, 1993. "It takes one second basically to put it [a seat belt] on. We know they work."

For Further Information

American Planning Association, March 1991.
Distribution, February 1993, p. 14.
New York Times, December 25, 1992, p. A24; March 16, 1993.
Rocky Mountain News, August 6, 1989.
Washington Post, January 7, 1993, p. A14.

Maggie Peña

Entrepreneur
Born January 29, 1959, Bogota, Colombia

"As Hispanics, we need to take a more aggressive leadership role with respect to finding and contributing to a solution to [the problems of Hispanic education]."

In 1988 Maggie Peña cofounded the National Society of Hispanic MBAs (NSHMBA). Since that time, she has worked to increase the number of Hispanic business students in graduate schools. She has also led the fight to improve Hispanic advancement in the business world. In 1991 Peña served as president of NSHMBA. During her presidency, she helped the society launch a scholarship program for Hispanic pupils. "Much has been written about the sad state of Hispanic education," she wrote in an article in *Hispanic*. "As Hispanics, we need to take a more aggressive leadership role with respect to finding and contributing to the solution to this problem."

Peña was born in 1959 in Bogota, Colombia. When she was seven years old, she moved with her family to Los Angeles, California. She attended school in Los Angeles until the eleventh grade, then completed her last two years of high school in Colombia. "My parents wanted me to get in touch with my cultural roots," she explained to Michelle Vachon in *Notable Hispanic American Women*.

In 1976 Peña won a four-year California state scholarship. She chose to attend

167

Immaculate Heart College in Los Angeles and graduated with a bachelor's degree in biology in 1980. For the next few years she worked as a biology lab assistant and as a high school chemistry teacher. She also managed to run her family's juice business.

MBA Provides Opportunities

At first, Peña planned on a career in scientific research. After working in a lonely laboratory for three years, however, she decided to change careers. She returned to school, enrolling in the University of California at Los Angeles. By 1986 she had earned a master of business administration (MBA) degree in marketing and finance.

The MBA opened up a world of opportunities for Peña. She worked as a financial analyst for the video division at Paramount Pictures Corporation. She managed Paramount's multimillion-dollar budget. "My experience in the corporate world opened my eyes to what was an unknown to me: the mysterious world of big business and big money," she told Vachon. Through her work at Paramount, Peña learned how to handle large business projects. More than that, she became confident in her own abilities.

Shares Skills with Hispanic Community

In 1988 Peña helped launch the NSHMBA. She and other Hispanics felt there was not enough support for Hispanics who wanted to study business in graduate school. By 1991 NSHMBA had grown to seven chapters across the country, and its members had raised $500,000 for educational opportunities for Hispanics. During her presidency of NSHMBA, Peña also established a summer enrichment program for junior high school students in Chicago, Los Angeles, and Washington, D.C.

"My work with the society proved extremely rewarding," Peña related to Vachon. "I developed a stronger sense of my Latino roots and discovered the tremendous network of Hispanic leaders nationwide." Peña believes that many people are more than willing to help others. They only need a person or an organization to show them where to begin. This is the function of a group like NSHMBA.

In 1991 Peña left Paramount Pictures to join her family's business—The Juice Fountain. Having taken over the reins of the business from her mother, Peña has expanded the business into three fresh-squeezed juice outlets in Los Angeles.

In addition to her work with NSHMBA, Peña also volunteers for at least five different charitable, fine arts, social, or political organizations. Her plans don't end here. In the future, she wants to work with youth groups to reduce school absenteeism and gang problems in Los Angeles. Peña also hopes to raise money to help poor children in Colombia, the country of her birth.

For Further Information

Hispanic, July 1991, p. 66; March 1992, p. 20.
Hispanic Business, February 1991, p. 21.
Notable Hispanic American Women, Gale Research, 1993, pp. 315-16.

Rosie Perez

Actress, dancer, choreographer
Born in Brooklyn, New York

"Hispanics, we're not even in the running. There are no roles. I'm stealing the roles written for nonminorities."

Rosie Perez

In just a few short years, Rosie Perez has switched from being a college student to a professional dancer to a busy actress. Her energy and talent for business have earned her jobs as a choreographer for a television show and a tour manager for a rap group. Most observers think she's racing along in a career fast-track, but Perez is not slowing down. "I'm very happy with the way things are going for me right now," she explained to Frank Spotnitz in *Entertainment Weekly,* "but I still feel like they're going too slow. I want it all."

Rosa Mary Perez was born in Bushwich, a mostly Puerto Rican district of Brooklyn. The exact year of her birth is her closely guarded secret. She'll only admit to being "under 25." She is the daughter of Ismael Serrano, a merchant marine, and Lydia Perez, who used to be a singer in Puerto Rico. When Perez was just a toddler, her mother placed her in a New York convent home. When she turned nine, she went to live with her father's sister, Anna.

Perez's family (which includes ten children) was on welfare, but that was no drawback to life in her neighborhood. "On the block where I grew up, everybody was in everybody's business," she told Mim Udovitch of *Vibe.* "You had no money so you couldn't go anywhere, and all your friends were there, so you just hung out. It was kind of cool because no one could act like they were better than anybody else...."

Dances Her Way onto Television

Although shy, Perez was a good student in school. She excelled at science, but had to take remedial speech classes—she called herself "Wosie" until sixth grade. As a teenager, she was also overweight, but she eventually slimmed down through diet and exercise. Perez moved to Los Angeles at age 18 to attend college, where she studied marine biology. While dancing one night in a Latino club in Los Angeles, she was spotted by a scout for the television show *Soul Train*. She was invited to become a dancer on the show and her entertainment career took off.

Perez soon danced her way into choreography. While she stayed with *Soul Train* for only a few shows, she made contacts that quickly led to other jobs. She created video and stage dance arrangements for singer Bobby Brown and rappers Al B. Sure, LL Cool J, and Heavy D & the Boyz. These in turn led her to the Fox television program *In Living Color*, where she became choreographer of the Fly Girls.

Moves to the Big Screen

During this period, while dancing at a Los Angeles club, Perez came to the attention of director Spike Lee. He offered her a part in his 1989 film, *Do the Right Thing*. She played the role of Tina, an unwed Puerto Rican mother with a quick temper. Some Hispanic groups criticized her for playing a stereotype, but she explained to Martha Frase-Blunt in *Hispanic* that she was playing an authentic role: "I was not portraying something that's not really out there."

Perez's performance soon brought her other projects. She appeared in television roles in such series as *21 Jump Street, Criminal Justice,* and *WIOU*. In almost all of these roles, however, she played the same type of character, and she was determined to branch out as an actress.

Her big break came with the 1992 hit film *White Men Can't Jump*. In the movie she played Woody Harrelson's feisty girlfriend, a character who originally was to have been a white woman from an Ivy League college.

After Ron Shelton, the film's writer-director, heard Perez audition for the role, he rewrote it for her, but only slightly. "I finally played someone," Perez told Charles Leerhsen in *Newsweek,* "who had it together, who wasn't a victim or messed up by the ghetto." In quick succession, Perez landed parts in *Night on Earth,* a small independent film, and *Untamed Heart,* starring Christian Slater and Marisa Tomei.

Lands First Starring Role

Perez played her very first starring role in *Fearless*, released in 1993. In the film, which also starred Jeff Bridges, Perez played a young mother who survives a plane crash but blames herself for her young son's death. Once again, the role was originally written for a white character, and noted actresses Jodie Foster and Winona Ryder both tried for the part. Once again, Perez had to fight for the role she eventually won. As Tony Bill, her director in *Untamed Heart*, explained to Leerhsen, "She has such a naturalness and a genuineness about her, that her way of doing something becomes the right way, the only way." Because Perez was so convincing in her role in *Fearless,* she was nominated for an Academy Award for best supporting actress.

Perez remains busy and in demand. She manages a female rhythm and blues group called 5 A.M., using a computer and fax machine to keep track of business deals. She also has begun directing music videos. In the summer of 1994 she was on the big screen again, playing opposite Nicholas Cage and Bridget Fonda in *It Could Happen to You*. Despite her recent successes, however, Perez has had to continue to fight against the narrow options open to Hispanic entertainers. "Hispanics, we're not even in the running," she told Udovitch. "There are no roles. I'm stealing the roles written for nonminorities."

For Further Information

Entertainment Weekly, April 3, 1992, p. 11.
Essence, October 1993, p. 63.
Hispanic, April 1993, pp. 14-16.
Newsweek, May 4, 1992, pp. 64-65.
Vibe, December 1993/January 1994, pp. 65-68.

Paloma Picasso

Fashion designer
Born April 19, 1949, Paris, France

"The most important thing is to know yourself. You should always be the same person. Style is how you conduct yourself, the silly things you do as well as everything else."

Paloma Picasso

Paloma Picasso is the daughter of Pablo Picasso, one of the twentieth century's most famous and influential artists. She has emerged from her famous father's shadow to establish an artistic reputation of her own—in the competitive world of fashion design. She has also launched an international company to sell her designs. Her work is whimsical and modern, and her use of color is dramatic and bold. Both reflect her own personality and style.

Picasso was born in Paris, France, in 1949. As the daughter of two artists, the Spanish Pablo Picasso and French Françoise Gilot, it is not surprising that she chose a career in the arts. She was named Paloma (Spanish for "dove") after the peace symbol her father created for the 95th World Peace Conference held in Paris at the time of her birth. Although Picasso's parents lived together for ten years, they never married because Pablo Picasso had been married before in Spain, and the law there did not permit divorce.

Pablo Picasso's genius and fame were an obstacle for his daughter. She was drawn to a career in art, but feared that her work would always be compared to that of her father. "From the time I was fourteen," she explained to Mary Batts Estrada in *Hispanic,* "I stopped drawing completely. I didn't want to hear, all day long, 'Oh, you're going to become a painter like your father.'" Instead, she decided to concentrate on fashion, and studied jewelry design in France.

Begins Designing for Yves St. Laurent

By the time she was a teenager, Picasso had already made her mark on the French fashion scene. She wore unusual, trendsetting clothes that she often bought in flea markets or antique stores. One of Picasso's friends at the time was the famous fashion designer Yves St. Laurent. In 1969 he asked her to design jewelry for his fashion show that year. Her creations began to be noticed, and soon she was asked to design bold pieces of costume jewelry for use in films and in stage plays.

Picasso stopped designing for a while after her father's death in 1973. She spent time arranging his estate. She also helped develop a new museum in his honor in Paris, the Musée Picasso. After meeting the Argentine playwright Rafael Lopez-Cambil, Picasso began to work again, designing costumes and sets for his productions. Their business relationship soon became personal and they married in 1978. Lopez-Cambil left the theater to become his wife's business partner.

According to Picasso, she provides the creative inspiration while her husband maps out the business plan. "I'm not disciplined at all," she admitted to an interviewer from *Harper's Bazaar.* "I'm very messy, yet I manage to do a great deal. I'm a terrible businesswoman, but Rafael, as a playwright, can envision all the parts and how to make them work together."

Expands Her Design Line

In 1980 Picasso designed her first collection of fine jewelry for Tiffany & Company in New York City. Her creations were chunky, large, bright, and expensive. She framed brilliant gems in blocks of gold, or hung large stones or pendants from simple cords. Her "hugs and kisses" jewelry (stylized Os and Xs in gold and silver) continue to be especially popular. They are often copied by other designers. Prices for Picasso's jewelry range from the low hundreds to a half million dollars.

Picasso introduced her own fragrance, called Paloma, in 1984. This was a natural move, since her grandfather, Emile Gilot, was a chemist and perfume manufacturer. Her scent took months to define, and she designed the packaging herself. The bottle is circle-shaped, and the surrounding red and black box is as bold and bright as some of Picasso's jewelry.

Picasso's face is familiar to many people because she often models her own fashions in full-page, glossy magazine ads. She makes a strong impression with her pale skin, dark hair, and deep-set, expressive eyes. Her looks are enhanced further by her own trademark deep red lipstick (only one color is available—*Mon Rouge,* "My Red").

Leads a Jet-Set Life

Since creating her perfume, Picasso has added accessories to her line of products. They include leather handbags, scarves, cosmetics, china, bathroom tiles, fabrics, and wallpaper. Her company has offices in New York, and stores in Paris and Tokyo. She travels regularly to Italy, where many of her products are made. To ease her busy life, Picasso speeds around the world in the supersonic Concorde jet. Her schedule is computerized, and she keeps a fax machine handy to send design ideas to her office.

Despite her hectic life, Picasso makes time to volunteer for a variety of Hispanic organizations. She devotes whatever time she can to help the fight against AIDS (Acquired Immune Deficiency Syndrome). Picasso tries to live by one simple rule: "The most important thing is to know yourself," she told Estrada. "You should always be the same person. Style is how you conduct yourself, the silly things you do as well as everything else."

For Further Information

Harper's Bazaar, December 1989, pp. 144-150; January 1991, pp. 123-26.
Hispanic, December 1988, pp. 28-33.
House Beautiful, March 1992, pp. 74-77.
Vogue, January 1990, pp. 190-97.

James Plunkett

Professional football quarterback
Born December 5, 1947, San Jose, California

"When a quarterback has been around, booed, cheered, and benched, he can feel good. He has lasted. Because every lasting quarterback experiences all of that in some order."

Perhaps better than anyone in professional sports, James William ("Jim") Plunkett has known the joy of victory and the

Jim Plunkett

agony of defeat. After a spectacular college career, he was named the National Football League's Rookie of the Year in 1971. Over the next few years, however, his career began to fall apart. He was injured several times and was traded. But Plunkett did not waver. He fought back to win the starting quarterback position with another team, eventually leading them to two Super Bowl victories. Plunkett explained to Tom Callahan in *Time,* "When a quarterback has been around, booed, cheered, and benched, he can feel good. He has lasted. Because every lasting quarterback experiences all of that in some order."

Plunkett was born in 1947 in San Jose, California. He was the youngest child and only son of blind Mexican American parents, William and Carmen Plunkett. His father managed a newsstand in San Jose, and the young Plunkett helped with family finances by selling newspapers and working as a grocery clerk and gas station attendant. Even in grade school, it was apparent that he was a great athlete. By junior high, he was a standout player in baseball, basketball, wrestling, and track, as well as football.

Plunkett led his high school team to championships and was offered a number of college football scholarships. He chose to attend Stanford University because it was close to home. He majored in political science and maintained a B average while setting records on the football field. During his junior year he threw passes for 2,671 yards and 20 touchdowns. He was named to the Associated Press's All-American second team, and won the Voit Memorial Trophy as the Pacific Athletic Conference's outstanding player.

Wins Heisman Trophy

During Plunkett's senior year at Stanford, he became the first major college team football player to surpass 7,000 yards on offense, setting the National Collegiate Athletic Association's career total offense mark. He led his team to victory in the Rose Bowl championship game on New Year's Day. At the end of that season, he won the Heisman Memorial Trophy, an annual award given to the best college football player in the United States.

After graduating from Stanford in 1971, Plunkett became the first pick in the National Football League (NFL) draft. He was chosen by the New England Patriots. He continued his spectacular play that first season, passing for 2,158 yards and 19 touchdowns. Even though the Patriots did not advance to postseason play, Plunkett capped off the season with the NFL Rookie of the Year award.

Career Spirals Downward

Then the bottom fell out. The Patriots were a weak team with an even weaker offensive line. Plunkett received no protection in the pocket and was battered by defensive linemen. Between 1972 and 1974, he was sacked 97 times. He underwent several knee and shoulder operations and lost his confidence. "The second year was miserable," he told Callahan. "I had never been on a losing team in my life, or experienced such negativism all around me." After Plunkett led the Patriots to a 3-11 season in 1975, the team lost its confidence in him. He was traded to the San Francisco 49ers.

Plunkett was pleased with the trade, as he was now closer to his recently widowed mother. His situation with the 49ers, however, soon proved worse than it had been with the Patriots. In a 1978 preseason game, he attempted 11 passes, completing none. San Francisco released him. "That's when I thought I was done," he explained to Rick Telander of *Sports Illustrated.* "I didn't think that I could play the game anymore."

Plunkett contemplated quitting the game he had excelled at his whole life, but his competitive drive was too strong. In 1978 he joined the Oakland (now Los Angeles) Raiders as a free agent. He spent the next two years sitting on the bench, letting both his injuries and his confidence heal.

Comeback of the Year

In the fifth game of the 1980 season, starting Raiders quarterback Dan Pastorini suffered a broken leg. Plunkett assumed control of the team and led it to victory throughout the rest of the season. He then guided the Raiders to victory in the 1981 Super Bowl. He was named the Super Bowl's Most Valuable Player and the NFL's 1980 Comeback Player of the Year.

Injured the following season, Plunkett lost his starting quarterback position. Again, he was forced to sit on the bench. Once again, he fought back. In 1983 he regained the quarterback spot and guided the Raiders to another successful season. In Super Bowl XVIII, he led the Raiders in a 38-9 blowout of the Washington Redskins. For Plunkett, it was the best season of his career: 230 completions for 1,935 yards and 20 touchdowns.

Injuries sidelined Plunkett over the next few years, and he was never able to recover. His football career came to an end when the Raiders released him in August 1988. Now retired, Plunkett passed for a total of 25,882 yards and 164 touchdowns during his long and inspiring career.

For Further Information

Buck, Ray, *Jim Plunkett, the Comeback Kid,* Children's Press, 1984.

Plunkett, Jim, *The Jim Plunkett Story: The Saga of a Man Who Came Back,* Arbor House, 1981.

Sports Illustrated, January 24, 1984, pp. 44-49.

Time, December 26, 1983, p. 78.

Juan Ponce de León

Spanish explorer
Born 1460, Santervas de Campos, Spain
Died July 1521, Havana, Cuba

"Beneath this stone repose the bones of the valiant Lion whose deeds surpassed the greatness of his name."—Inscription on gravestone

Juan Ponce de León was the first European to visit Florida and explore its coastline. He is also remembered for his exploration and subsequent appointment as governor of Puerto Rico. Although a legend claims that he came to the New World in search of the mythical "fountain of youth," it is more likely that Ponce de León—like most Spanish explorers—came looking for gold and other riches.

Born in 1460 into a poor but noble family in Spain, Ponce de León spent his boyhood as a page (a young person in training) to a powerful nobleman. During adolescence, he began his military education. He later fought with the Spanish army against the Moors (Muslims) in southern Spain. His bravery led to an assignment to travel with Christopher Columbus on his second voyage to the New World in 1493.

In 1502 Ponce de León traveled to Hispaniola (the Caribbean island presently occupied by the Dominican Republic and Haiti). In 1504 he helped stop a revolt by Indians in the province of Higuey, on the eastern part of the island. As a reward, King

Juan Ponce de León

The "Fountain of Youth"

Ponce de León was removed from this appointment in 1511 when Diego Columbus (the son of Christopher) was given authority over all of Spain's possessions in the Caribbean. By this time, Ponce de León was a wealthy man and accepted his loss of power calmly. Having heard stories of a rich island called Bimini just north of Cuba, he sought the right to find and settle the island. Bimini supposedly contained a mysterious spring that restored youth to all who drank its waters. Most historians don't believe Ponce de León actually believed the myth. Many stories, legends, and romantic tales, however, have persisted about his quest for the spring. It is more likely that Ponce de León was simply searching for more wealth in the New World.

In 1513 Ponce de León left Puerto Rico with three ships and sailed north to San Salvador. Hunting for Bimini, he and his men moved on until they sighted land. When they went ashore, Ponce de León named the place *Florida* ("flowery" in Spanish). It is unclear whether he chose this name because of the colorful beauty of the land, or because the landing coincided with the feast of Easter, which is called *la pascua florida* in Spanish. In the name of King Ferdinand, he took possession of the new land near the present-day city of St. Augustine on the eastern coast of Florida.

Discovers Gulf Stream

Ponce de León's expedition then headed south, but its boats were slowed by a heavy current. This was the Gulf Stream. The discovery of this strong current opened a new route for Spanish travel from the Caribbean

Ferdinand of Spain made him governor of Higuey.

A few years later, an Indian from the neighboring island of Borinquen (later renamed Puerto Rico by the Spanish) arrived in Higuey with a large nugget of gold. The Spanish were always hoping to find the precious metal, and Ponce de León immediately led an expedition to investigate the island. His army conquered the island, and he was named governor of the new Spanish possession of Puerto Rico.

to North America. The Spanish ships dropped anchor at points along the shore, but several unfriendly encounters with Native Americans encouraged Ponce de León to continue on. He and his men followed the shoreline around the southern tip of Florida and past the Florida Keys. Ponce de León then came upon a group of islands where he and his men captured 170 turtles. As a result, he named the islands *Tortugas* ("turtles" in Spanish). This small group of islands are presently known as the Dry Tortugas.

The expedition sailed north along the Gulf coast of Florida as far as Sanibel Island, then turned and headed back toward Cuba. Ponce de León sent one ship on in search of Bimini. That ship reached Andros Island in the present-day Bahamas. Upon rejoining Ponce de León, that ship's navigator admitted he found no "fountain of youth."

Ponce de León returned to Puerto Rico where he was again involved in settling Indian rebellions. After restoring order, he sailed back to Spain where King Ferdinand rewarded him for his explorations by naming him Captain General. He was then ordered to continue his search for Bimini. The king also commanded him to start a settlement on Florida, which the Spanish believed was an island.

Fatally Wounded by Native Americans

Ponce de León returned to Puerto Rico, where he stayed five years before setting out on a final adventure. In 1521 he undertook a second journey to find Bimini with two ships, about two hundred men, fifty horses, and many domestic animals. Included in his group were several priests to help spread

Woodcut of Ponce de León searching for the Fountain of Youth

Christianity among the native people. After landing on the west coast of Florida, the group was immediately attacked by Native Americans. Ponce de León was wounded and taken back to his ship, which then sailed to Cuba. There Ponce de León died in July 1521. His body was shipped to Puerto Rico for burial.

Ponce de León died without really knowing the importance of his discoveries. The fearless warrior and explorer was laid to rest under the altar in a San Juan church. Today, many places in Puerto Rico and Florida bear his name. The inscription on his gravestone reads, "Beneath this stone repose the bones of the valiant Lion (*León* is "lion" in Spanish) whose deeds surpassed the greatness of his name."

For Further Information

Blassingame, Wyatt, *Ponce de León,* Chelsea House, 1991.

Hispanic, December 1990, p. 54.

King, Ethel M., *The Fountain of Youth and Juan Ponce de León,* T. Guaus' Sons, 1963.

Peck, Douglas T., *Ponce de León and the Discovery of Florida: The Man, the Myth, and the Truth,* Pogo Press, 1993.

Tito Puente

Musician
Born April 20, 1923, New York, New York

"I don't like titles. If you're called the king of something—the King of Boogaloo or the King of Rock—once the music dies, then the king dies, too."

For years, Tito Puente has been known as *El Rey*—the King. He would rather be known as a regular musician. "I don't like titles," he told Larry Birnbaum in *Down Beat.* "If you're called the king of something—the King of Boogaloo or the King of Rock—once the music dies, then the king dies, too." Puente's reign as the "King of Latin Music," however, is well assured. His career as a bandleader, composer, and percussionist has spanned almost 50 years, during which time he has recorded over 100 albums—a feat unmatched in the music industry.

Puente was born Ernest Anthony Puente, Jr., in 1923 in the Spanish Harlem section of New York City. His parents, Ernest Anthony and Ercilia Puente, had immigrated to the United States from Puerto Rico just a few years before. From a young age, Puente knew he wanted to be a musician: "I was always banging on cans and boxes," he told Birnbaum. His musical education started with piano lessons. After five years, he began taking trap drum lessons at the New York School of Music. In addition to his music classes, Puente received formal training in dance.

Not all of Puente's musical influences and training came from a classroom. While growing up, he listened for hours to the music of big band leaders such as Artie Shaw, Duke Ellington, and Benny Goodman. When he was older, his father took him to weekend dances, where he sat in with various bands. He especially enjoyed accompanying the new and innovative Latin bands, whose music was based on Afro-Cuban rhythms. During his apprenticeship, Puente learned to play the timbales—a pair of tuned, open-bottomed drums played with sticks. They were to become the instrument of his career.

Influenced by Cuban Music

At the age of 15, Puente dropped out of high school and traveled to Miami Beach to play with a Latin band. At the time, travel to Cuba from the United States was allowed, and Puente went there often. "I picked up a lot of music, listened a lot to the radio, and met a lot of musicians," he related in the interview with Birnbaum. After a few years, he traveled back to New York City to play with Latin bands, which were quickly gaining popularity there.

During World War II, Puente served three years in the U.S. Navy aboard an aircraft carrier. When he could, he jammed with other musicians on the ship. He also taught

Tito Puente

himself how to play the saxophone during his off-hours. After his discharge in 1945, he enrolled in the prestigious Juilliard School of Music in New York City on the G.I. Bill (money given by the U.S. government to members of the military to attend school). While at Juilliard, Puente studied composition and orchestration. The leading Latin orchestras of that time soon began to play his compositions and arrangements. In 1949 he formed his own orchestra, the Picadilly Boys.

Leads the Mambo Craze

In the late 1940s and early 1950s, a new type of dance music swept across the eastern United States. It combined Latin beats with elements of American jazz and would later evolve into a musical form known as *salsa.* (Puente was a leader in the creation of the salsa sound, which reached new heights in the 1970s after fusing with harder-edged rock sounds.) In the 1950s, the early form of this rich musical blend was being played in ballrooms in big cities throughout the United States, where people danced the *mambo,* a rhythmic Cuban dance set to horns and various percussive instruments. Puente's orchestra, with its shrill horn section and his heavy drums, became the greatest mambo group in the nation. Its home was the famed Palladium Ballroom in New York City, a place where everyone danced together, regardless of ethnicity. "The place was a big melting pot," Puente recalled in an interview with Lorenzo Chavez for *Hispanic.* "Jews, Italians, Irish, Blacks, Puerto Ricans, Cubans, you name it. Everyone was equal under the roof of the Palladium."

Puente and his orchestra always tried to bring fresh music to their listeners. When new compositions came out of Cuba, Puente arranged them to fit his group's style. Aside from playing in ballrooms across the country, the orchestra also played in jazz clubs. "I was always trying to find a marriage between Latin music and jazz," Puente told Birnbaum. "I was trying to play jazz but not lose the Latin-American authenticity." Over the years, Puente has recorded with such jazz greats as Lionel Hampton, Woody Herman, and Dizzy Gillespie.

In the late 1950s another blend of musical styles was also arising—rock 'n' roll. It soon changed national music tastes, and the popularity of Latin dance music declined. Throughout the 1960s, Latin orchestras disbanded or switched to playing other musical styles. But, even though he didn't have the audience he once had, Puente continued to play his trademark music in clubs and record album after album during this period.

Rocker Revives His Career

Puente's career received a boost in 1970 when rocker Carlos Santana (see **Carlos Santana**) and his band recorded "Oye Como Va," one of Puente's early compositions. The song became a hit for Santana. In the process, it also introduced Puente and his Latin jazz to a whole new audience. Sales of his albums increased and his popularity grew. In 1978, for his recording *Homenaje a Beny More,* he was given his first of several Grammy awards, the music industry's highest honor. The next year, President Jimmy Carter invited Puente and his group to perform at the White House. It was the first time a Latin orchestra had played before a U.S. president.

Since that time, Puente's public exposure has increased steadily. In 1990 he was awarded a star on the Hollywood Walk of Fame, joining a select list of other Hispanics so honored by the entertainment industry. In addition, he has recorded with a variety of pop stars and other musicians, and has made guest appearances on the large and small screens. In 1992 he played a small role in *The Mambo Kings Play Songs of Love,* the film adaptation of Oscar Hijuelos's (see **Oscar Hijuelos**) Pulitzer Prize-winning book. Puente also served as the film's musical director.

As Puente's celebrity status has grown, so has his generosity and social concern. In 1989 he staged a benefit concert that raised $150,000 to help Puerto Rican victims of

Hurricane Hugo. He also started the Tito Puente Scholarship Fund at Juilliard. The fund makes it possible for minority students in New York City to receive a musical education. Puente explained to Birnbaum that he started the fund to give "a young Latin percussionist an incentive to learn how to read music.... It's not only what you learn in the streets—you've really got to go and study."

For Further Information

Américas, November/December 1990, pp. 56-57.
Down Beat, January 1984, pp. 27-29+; May 1991, pp. 20-21.
Hispanic, March 1991, pp. 46-48.
New York, June 15, 1992, pp. 10A-13A.
Village Voice, March 14, 1977, p. 39.

Anthony Quinn

Anthony Quinn

Actor, artist
Born April 21, 1915, Chihuahua, Mexico

"His Latin looks were not of the soft, gleaming, sensuous kind—more like the glare of the bandido who would kill you for making fun of him."—David Denby, Premiere

In the 1940s and 1950s, Anthony Quinn made his mark in Hollywood playing Latin roles in such movies as *Viva Zapata!,* the 1952 film about the Mexican revolutionary Emiliano Zapata (see **Emiliano Zapata**). Since that time, however, Quinn has become one of the few but increasing number of Hispanic actors whose careers have not been limited to Hispanic roles. His most famous role came in the 1964 film *Zorba the Greek,* in which he played the title character. He also played a biblical character in *Barrabas* (1961), an Arab in *Lawrence of Arabia* (1962), and a Russian pope in *The Shoes of the Fisherman* (1968).

Quinn was born in the Mexican state of Chihuahua in 1915. At that time, the country was in the grip of the Mexican Revolution. To avoid the conflict, Quinn's Mexican mother and Irish Mexican father smuggled him to the United States as an infant. When he was nine, his father was killed in an automobile accident. The young Quinn then had to help support his mother and younger sister. He worked an assortment of jobs, including custodian, boxer, and migrant farm worker. Unable to finish his high school education, he continued to learn through reading and travel.

Begins Acting during the Depression

During the Great Depression (a period in the 1930s when the nation suffered from an extremely slow economy and widespread unemployment), Quinn joined a Federal Theater Project. This program was one of many sponsored by the government at the time to help people find work. While involved with the project, Quinn came to realize his love for acting. He then polished his acting skills by working with local theater groups. In 1937 he made his motion picture debut, playing a Native American in *The Plainsman,* directed by the famous Cecil B. DeMille.

Quinn then married Katherine DeMille, the adopted daughter of DeMille. For the next ten years he managed to find steady work in supporting roles portraying Native Americans, Latin lovers, Mexican villains, and other ethnic types. In 1947 he became a U.S. citizen. That same year he made his Broadway (New York) stage debut.

Award-Winning Roles

In 1952 Quinn finally achieved star status with his role in *Viva Zapata!* The screenplay was written by Nobel Prize-winning novelist John Steinbeck. The film presents the life of Emiliano Zapata as he leads the peasant revolt in Mexico beginning in 1910. Marlon Brando portrayed Zapata while Quinn portrayed Zapata's brother, Eufemio Zapata.

Quinn's flawless performance in the film earned him an Academy award in 1952 for best supporting actor.

At that time, Hollywood often cast Hispanic actors for their leading-man looks, but Quinn was cast for his acting ability. "[His] Latin looks were not of the soft, gleaming, sensuous kind—more like the glare of the bandido who would kill you for making fun of him," David Denby wrote in *Premiere.*

In 1956 Quinn received his second Academy award for a best supporting actor performance in *Lust for Life.* The absorbing film biography presents the life of Vincent van Gogh from his first paintings to his death. Kirk Douglas played the tortured Dutch painter in the film. Quinn gave a stunning performance as the French painter Paul Gauguin.

Portrays Zorba

Perhaps Quinn's best-known film is *Zorba the Greek.* He seemed well-suited to the role of a crude but sensitive Greek peasant—a simple, intelligent man who accepts life's ups and downs and makes the most of them. Based on the novel by Nikolai Kazantzakis, the film follows the talkative, outgoing Zorba as he meets a young English writer. During the course of the film, Zorba teaches the serious young man to accept and enjoy the simple things in life. In a climactic and symbolic scene, the two link arms and do a boisterous peasant dance on the beach. Quinn's performance was again recognized by Hollywood: he received an Academy award nomination for best actor in 1965.

Quinn has acted in more than 100 films. Between 1983 and 1986, he toured the country in a musical version of *Zorba.* Although he underwent successful heart bypass surgery in 1990, he continues to work. In the early 1990s he starred in such notable films as *Revenge,* with Kevin Costner, and *The Last Action Hero,* with Arnold Schwarzenegger.

Like some of the characters he has played, Quinn has lived an expansive life. After divorcing his first wife, he married his second wife, Iolanda, in 1961. He is the father of 12 children. Along with acting, he expresses his creativity through art. He is an accomplished painter and sculptor who has had several very successful one-man exhibitions of his work. In 1972 he published his autobiography, *The Original Sin.*

For Further Information

Amdur, Melissa, *Anthony Quinn,* Chelsea House, 1993.
People, September 6, 1993, p. 80.
Premiere, September 1992, pp. 43-45.
Quinn, Anthony, *The Original Sin: A Self-Portrait,* Little, Brown, 1972.

Diego Rivera

Diego Rivera

Artist
Born December 8, 1886, Guanajuato, Mexico
Died November 24, 1957, San Angel, Mexico

"Rivera devoted his artistic talents to the portrayal of injustice toward the workers of Mexico and other countries."

D iego Rivera was a famous Mexican painter whose large-scale, intricate murals tell the history of his people. Combining symbols of his own strong political beliefs with unmistakable elements of folk art, Rivera created works that champion the cause of struggling workers throughout the world. Although some of his paintings were destroyed by people who disagreed with his politics, most of his works remain for the enjoyment and education of present and future generations of artists and art lovers.

Rivera was born in 1886 in the city of Guanajuato, located almost 200 miles northwest of Mexico City. His parents, Maria and Diego Rivera, had invested much of their money in the silver mines surrounding Guanajuato, but the mines had long since given up all their silver. Left with little money, Rivera's father found work as a grade school teacher and then as a local government official.

Rivera's artistic talent surfaced early. By the age of three, he was drawing all over the house—on furniture, on walls, in record books, and on any loose papers. To stop his son from marking up the entire house, the elder Rivera put canvases on the walls of a small room in their home. Young Diego was free to draw on anything in his very first studio.

While Rivera was growing up, Mexico was governed by Porfirio Diaz. Under his tyrannical rule, the rich landowners in Mexico prospered while the poor and the lower classes suffered. Rivera's father started a weekly newspaper in Guanajuato that called attention to the plight of the poor. In turn, the newspaper came to the attention of inhabitants of Guanajuato who were loyal to Diaz, and the Rivera family was forced to move to Mexico City in 1893.

Inspired by Mexican Folk Art

A year later, Rivera began his education. His mother was a devout Catholic and insisted he attend a parochial school (one governed by a religious body). Although he did not share his mother's religious convictions, Rivera did extremely well in the school, graduating with honors in 1898. In addition, for two years he took art classes during the evenings at the famous Academy of San Carlos. After his graduation from grammar school, he decided to attend the academy full time. Here he improved his technique, learning the basic laws of drawing; he also learned and adhered to the strict rules of classical European art. Rivera's own artistic tastes, however, were drawn more to the free-flowing native designs and folk art of Mexico.

In 1903 Rivera took part in a student protest against the Diaz government. All the students involved were expelled from the Academy of San Carlos and then later readmitted, but Rivera never returned. He had been unhappy with the academy's insistence on an almost photographic realism in the students' work. Wandering the countryside, he painted and drew what he saw. Although he had very little confidence in his work, others quickly recognized his talent.

In 1907—with money from sales of his works and from admirers like Teodoro A. Dehesa, the governor of the Mexican state of Vera Cruz—Rivera sailed to Europe to study the works of the artistic masters. He traveled to Spain, Belgium, Holland, England, and Italy before finally settling in Paris. For the first time in his life, he read a vast number of books. The writings of Karl Marx, the Prussian social philosopher whose ideas led to the development of communism, made a lasting impression on him. (Communism is a political theory based on the elimination of private ownership of property and the formation of a classless society.) Among artists, Rivera was greatly influenced by the works of Paul Cézanne of France, and Francisco Goya and El Greco, both of Spain. He copied their works, learning their choices of color and line. Throughout his travels in Europe, however, his love of Mexico remained evident in his own works.

Begins His Mexican Murals

In 1922 Alvaro Obregón, then president of Mexico, encouraged Rivera to return to his homeland to participate in a national popular art movement. Government leaders invited him to paint murals on many public buildings. These murals allowed Rivera a chance to depict the new ideas that he had developed in Europe about the history and the social struggles of Mexicans. He pictured the cruelties of the Spanish conquistadors, the heroes of the Mexican Revolution, the sorry state of the nation's lower-class farm workers (commonly referred to as "the peasantry"), and the need for radical changes in society.

Rivera then spent some time in the mid-1920s traveling throughout the rural areas of Mexico. He studied the native history, life, and culture of his country. His work developed a bold, earthy warmth and a simple folk style that was appropriate for his subjects. Rivera's paintings did not demean the peasants, but gave them a proud and intelligent air. Filled with religious and historical imagery, his paintings told fascinating stories. Most art critics agree that Rivera created his greatest works during this period. In 1926, at the Agricultural School in the city of Chapingo, he painted a mural on 30 panels that tells the story of Mexican land reform and depicts scenes of a better society where common laborers, the middle class, and government come together.

During the 1930s Rivera was invited to produce work in the United States. Officials in several American cities asked him to paint murals on the walls of their public buildings. In 1931 he completed *Allegory of California,* a 30-foot-high mural at the San Francisco Stock Exchange. The following year, he painted a fascinating mural depicting the history of the automobile industry on the walls of the Garden Court in the Detroit Institute of Arts. After *Detroit Industry* was completed, some observers demanded that it be removed, saying it depicted automobile workers merely as part of the large

machines. Workers in Detroit, however, defended the mural and it was saved.

Rockefeller Mural Destroyed

Rivera's next piece met a sad fate. In 1932 the artist began work on a mural for the RCA Building in Rockefeller Center in New York City. Even before the painting was completed, it created controversy. New Yorkers were furious to see Rivera include in his mural of workers and leaders a portrait of Vladimir Lenin, the Russian revolutionary and founder of the Soviet Union. The Rockefeller family asked Rivera to remove Lenin's face, but he refused. Rivera was then dismissed from the project and the mural was destroyed. Undaunted, Rivera returned to Mexico City in 1934 and recreated the mural in the Palace of Fine Arts.

Rivera's work continued to create controversy, even in his own country. In 1948 his mural for the Del Prado Hotel in Mexico City caused a riot in the streets around the building. This time the anger was directed at a scroll in the mural that contained the words "God does not exist." Catholic students raided the hotel and damaged the work. The mural was eventually restored and in 1960 moved to the main lobby of the Del Prado.

Rivera continued to be artistically and politically active until his death from heart failure on November 24, 1957. He had devoted his artistic talents to the portrayal of injustice toward the workers of Mexico and other countries. His technique—mixing soft lines and earthen tones with sharp lines and harsh colors—had an enormous influence on art in Mexico and the United States in the twentieth century. Rivera's murals and paintings are carefully preserved wherever they have survived around the world.

For Further Information

Cockcroft, James, *Diego Rivera,* Chelsea House, 1991.

Detroit Institute of Arts Founders Society, *Diego Rivera: A Retrospective,* Norton, 1986.

Hargrove, Jim, *Diego Rivera: Mexican Muralist,* Children's Press, 1990.

Rivera, Diego, *My Art, My Life,* Citadel Press, 1960.

Wolfe, Bertram D., *The Fabulous Life of Diego Rivera,* Stein and Day, 1960.

Geraldo Rivera

Broadcast journalist and talk-show host
Born July 4, 1943, New York City

"I invented sleaze.... But I'm also the guy who democratized the news-gathering process in this country. I brought passion and compassion to journalism."

Geraldo Rivera is one of the most controversial television journalists in the business. He has worked as a lawyer, reporter, writer, and talk-show host. Critics question his objectivity and unorthodox style of reporting. Even so, Rivera's programs have drawn large audiences, making him one of the most visible and successful Hispanics in the media and entertainment field.

Rivera was born in 1943 in New York City to Cruz Rivera and Lilly Friedman. As the son of a Puerto Rican father and Jewish mother, Rivera had a difficult time handling his two distinct identities while he was growing up. He was not a great student in high school—he was more interested in sports and street gangs. Rivera spent two years in the U.S. Merchant Marine Corps before attending college.

When Rivera attended the University of Arizona, he felt especially isolated. He tried to fit in with the other students, but was never accepted. He even tried to hide his ethnic identity, going by the name Jerry Rivers. Still, he was not accepted because of the way he looked and spoke.

After graduating from the University of Arizona, Rivera studied law at Brooklyn Law School. He eventually received his law degree from the University of Pennsylvania. He then focused on helping the poor. He worked for the Harlem Assertion of Rights and for the Community Action for Legal Services. For a short while he represented a gang of Spanish-speaking youths called the Young Lords. He convinced the gang to turn their energy away from fighting and violence to more useful projects such as organizing day care centers. However, Rivera grew restless with the slow process of law and turned to a flashier job.

Switches from Law to Journalism

In 1970 Rivera took advantage of new minority hiring policies and applied for a job as a newscaster with a television station in New York City. For three months he studied journalism intensively at Columbia University's Graduate School of Journalism. Rivera then made his debut on the station's *Eyewitness News* program. As a rookie reporter he was assigned to routine stories such as fashion shows and charity functions.

One day, while on the way to cover a feature story, he encountered a drug addict who was threatening to jump from a rooftop. Rivera tape-recorded a dramatic and emotional plea for help from the addict's brother while the camera crew filmed the entire event. The story was aired on the evening news. The gripping story captured the attention of the station's producers, and Rivera was assigned more serious stories afterward.

Rivera's popularity grew quickly, especially among young viewers, and he received honors and awards for his work. Rivera gained national publicity for his 1972 news story, "Willowbrook: A Report on How It Is and Why It Doesn't Have To Be That Way." He had smuggled a camera crew into the Willowbrook State School for the Mentally Retarded in New York to expose the terrible conditions in which the patients lived. The report was emotional and heartbreaking, and catapulted Rivera to celebrity.

Reaction was strong to the Willowbrook story. Donations poured in, and Rivera helped create a fundraising project to benefit mentally disabled people. He volunteered many hours working for the group he named "One-to-One." Today he is chairman of the association.

Rivera explained his reasons for donating his time and effort to helping others in an article he wrote for *Esquire:* "I love being a newsman. Given enormous power and responsibility by the network, I have tried to use my position to make the world a slightly better place.... Sometimes the reporter has to become involved in helping society change the things he is complaining about."

Geraldo Rivera

Reporting Style Is Aggressive and Subjective

This desire to change the world has earned Rivera both praise and criticism. He has been accused of exaggerating facts and distorting the news he reports. Also, he has been criticized for being too involved in the stories he reports. While interviewing people, he often reacts with emotion and tears, drawing attention toward himself. Many in the national news establishment are embarrassed and angered by his lack of objectivity. They say he injects his own opinion into stories, which prevents him from presenting issues fairly.

Rivera disagrees with his critics' idea of what makes a good newsperson. For him, subjectivity means caring. "Soul is the missing ingredient in television journalism," he wrote in a *TV Guide* article. "Coolness has become synonymous with objectivity, aloofness with professionalism. [Network news] is seldom courageous or involved and almost never passionate."

During the 1970s and early 1980s, Rivera traveled the globe aggressively for ABC News, covering many political and social events that have shaped our world. He gave on-site reports from such areas as war-torn Afghanistan and the crime-ridden streets of Guatemala. In 1983 he covered the Israeli-Palestinian conflict from Tripoli in northwest Lebanon. While sitting safely in a car, Rivera and his crew saw an explosion wound a young Palestinian soldier. Rivera raced from the car, pulled the soldier to safety, tended his wound, then helped him into a nearby ambulance. Although the story aired on the evening news, network executives cut Rivera out of the tape that was shown.

The incident soured the relationship between Rivera and executives at ABC. Over the next two years, the argument over his brand of personal journalism intensified. Finally, in 1985, ABC fired him.

The Opening of Al Capone's Vault

Rivera soon found that being let go was the best thing that could have happened to his career. In 1986 he began producing and hosting a series of news specials. The first was called "The Mystery of Al Capone's Vault." After a two-hour buildup, nothing more than a few dusty bottles were discovered in the late mobster's vault. Although Rivera was embarrassed by the incident, a huge audience had watched the live TV show, leading to calls for him to lead other specials.

In 1987 Rivera launched his hour-long talk show, *Geraldo*. The show typically focuses on offbeat, even lurid topics. *Geraldo* earns the same praise and criticism that Rivera's work has always attracted. In 1988, during a show titled "Teen Hatemongers," a violent fight broke out between the guests—white racists and black activists. Fists, bodies, and chairs flew across the stage. Even members of the audience joined in. Rivera attempted to calm the free-for-all, but received a broken nose when he was hit by a chair. Police were called in to subdue the crowd, and a dramatic, bloody Rivera concluded the show.

Critics call Rivera's work "tabloid" or "trash TV." Rivera simply points to his growing audiences, and insists he is giving them useful information. He admits that soap-opera themes dominate *Geraldo,* but says his treatment of such topics raises them to a level of news best understood by everyone. "I invented sleaze.... But I'm also the guy who democratized the news-gathering process in this country," Rivera was quoted as saying in the *Detroit Free Press*. "I brought passion and compassion to journalism."

For Further Information

Detroit Free Press, September 19, 1994.
Esquire, April 1986.
Rivera, Geraldo, *Exposing Myself,* Bantam, 1991.
TV Guide, April 18, 1987; March 26, 1988.

Gloria Rodríguez

Founder and president of Avance Family
Support and Educational Program
Born July 9, 1948, San Antonio, Texas

*"Children from a strong family [have] a better
chance at surviving. Parents must be in the
front line of preparing kids for success."*

Teaching parents how to raise their children was unheard of in 1973. Yet Gloria Rodríguez turned the idea into a career by providing low-income Hispanic mothers in Texas with basic parenting skills. As founder and director of Avance (Spanish for "advance"), Rodríguez has helped thousands of women break the cycle of poverty, ignorance, and abuse through classes and special programs. Avance is considered a unique national success story among social service organizations in the United States.

Born in 1948, Rodríguez grew up in a poor Hispanic neighborhood in San Antonio, Texas. Her father, Julian Garza, died when she was two. Her mother, Lucy Villegas Salazar, was left to rear eight children alone. To help raise money for the family, Rodríguez and her sisters sold their mother's homemade jewelry. At age nine, Rodríguez got a job cleaning a neighbor's house. When she started high school, she worked as a clerk in a department store. Rodríguez excelled in school. A popular cheerleader and beauty queen, she graduated in 1967 with good grades.

Rodríguez wanted to be a teacher, but she knew she could not afford college. Her life changed when she was selected for a possible scholarship from Project Teacher Excellence. This government program was designed to give disadvantaged students a chance to study bilingual education. In exchange, the students chosen are expected to return to their communities to teach. Rodríguez competed against 300 other students for the scholarship. She almost lost her chance when her high school principal wouldn't recommend her—he did not think she was "college material." Rodríguez persuaded the committee to give her a chance, and she set out to prove the principal wrong.

"I knew college would be difficult," Rodríguez explained to a reporter for the *West Side Sun.* "Other college students were better prepared academically and could express themselves better in the English language." To help get through the troubling times at school, Rodríguez relied on her deep religious faith. She credits her grandfather, who came to live with the family after her father died, with giving her this faith. "I went daily to the chapel to pray," she told the same reporter. "I vowed that if I did well, I would use my training to help others."

Links Parenting to School Success

Rodríguez completed her bachelor of arts degree in elementary education and bilingual education from Our Lady of the Lake University in 1970. Three years later she earned her master of education degree. She was then hired to be San Antonio's first bilingual teacher. Her first class was a group of 35 first graders labeled "problem learners." She found that her low-income students had difficulties in Spanish as well as in

Gloria Rodríguez

English. She remembered that her own family had been poor, yet it had managed to instill respect, independence, and determination in herself and her siblings.

"It was like a light bulb went on: it all starts with the family," Rodríguez told a reporter for the *Dallas Morning News*. "Children from a strong family [have] a better chance at surviving. Parents must be in the front line of preparing kids for success."

From then on, Rodríguez focused on educating parents. She believed that education begins at home—the first and most important teachers are parents. When she found out that a company was willing to fund a new education program called Avance in San Antonio, she went after the job. Rodríguez was immediately hired as the director. She set up her first program in the Mirasol Housing Projects, a few blocks from her childhood home.

Survival Training for Families

Avance had humble beginnings. Rodríguez and three assistants went from door to door encouraging parents to take part in the program. A handful of skeptical women signed up. Almost all of them were high school dropouts and single mothers living on public assistance. Rodríguez discovered that family problems often started with overwhelming financial and social conditions. Many parents are under the stress of simply trying to survive. Sometimes they take their fear and despair out on their children.

Avance's nine-month program gives mothers and their preschool children a support system that many of them have never known. The parents and their children meet every week for three hours in a clean and friendly environment. While the children play in supervised groups, their mothers learn about child development, discipline techniques, problem-solving skills, nutrition, and safety. Together, parents and children take field trips, plant gardens, build friendships, and learn to communicate.

"This is a prevention program," Rodríguez told an interviewer for *Vista* magazine. "Before the 1970s, all treatment went to the child. But you can't separate the child from the environment, so you start with the family."

Expands Avance Programs

Rodríguez persuaded area businesses, governments, and charities to contribute money to Avance. She expanded its programs to include prenatal (before birth) services for pregnant women and a Fatherhood Project similar to the mothers' classes. In addition, Rodríguez had Avance offer literacy (reading) programs and job placement services for parents.

Rodríguez supervises a staff of 120 (many of them Avance graduates) and operates a $2.7 million annual budget. Avance has sites in the Texas cities of San Antonio, Houston, and Brownsville. Future programs are planned for Dallas, El Paso, and Puerto Rico. Many national and international dignitaries have visited Avance, including former U.S. First Lady Barbara Bush and England's Prince Charles.

Rodríguez married engineer Salvador C. Rodríguez, Jr., in 1972. The couple has three children. Over the years, Rodríguez has continued her own education, earning a doctorate degree in early childhood education from the University of Texas at Austin in 1991. She has received numerous honors and awards for her work, including the Temple Award for Creative Altruism from the National Institute of Noetic (relating to the intellect) Science in 1993. Rodríguez has also been inducted into both the San Antonio and the Texas Halls of Fame.

For Further Information

Business Week, February 20, 1989, p. 151.
Dallas Morning News, February 16, 1992, p. 41A.
Vista, May 20, 1990, p. 16.
West Side Sun (San Antonio), August 30, 1979; October 5, 1989; May 16, 1991.

Juan "Chi Chi" Rodríguez

Professional golfer
Born October 23, 1935, Río Piedras, Puerto Rico

"I just feel like I'm in heaven, the peace of God comes over me, when these kids touch me on the shoulder and say, 'Uncle Chi Chi.'"

Juan "Chi Chi" Rodríguez is famous for his successful golf game and his entertaining attitude on the course. Fans love to follow the Puerto Rican senior player to witness his playing skills and to laugh at his jokes. His charitable efforts are equally impressive. He helps run a foundation for troubled children in Florida, contributes to a children's hospital in Puerto Rico, and gives golf clinics for underprivileged children.

Rodríguez was born in 1935 in Río Piedras, Puerto Rico, to Juan and Modesta Rodríguez. He grew up in poverty. His father was a laborer who worked in sugarcane fields and never earned more than $18 a week to support his family of six children. Once, when he had a heart attack, he was fired from his job. Rodríguez claims that his small size (5 feet 7 inches) is a result of childhood illnesses caused by poor nutrition.

While growing up, Rodríguez was more interested in sports than in school (he earned his childhood nickname from his hero, Puerto Rican baseball star Chi Chi Flores). Lacking the money to buy his own golf equipment, he took a job as a golf course

Juan "Chi Chi" Rodríguez

caddy. For practice, he hit tin cans with a guava (tree) stick.

When he turned 19, Rodríguez enlisted in the U.S. Army. During his two-year service, he joined the army's golf team to keep up his skills. After returning to Puerto Rico, he worked as an orderly in a psychiatric clinic helping to care for the mentally ill. "It gave me more satisfaction than winning golf tournaments," Rodríguez related to Doris Lee McCoy of the *Saturday Evening Post*. "Of course, I wanted to do better in life, so I went into golf after that."

Begins Professional Golfing Career

In 1957 Rodríguez got a job at the Dorado Beach Country Club and took lessons to improve his game. By 1960 he was good enough to join the Professional Golf Association (PGA). Three years later he won his first tournament, the Denver Open. He went on to enjoy a moderately successful, 25-year career with the PGA, earning over one million dollars. His last tournament victory came in 1979. After that, his career went downhill, and he contemplated quitting. "Older players cannot compete with young guys," he explained to Ira Wolfman in *New Choices*. "The worst thing you can do is play and have someone feel sorry for you."

Rodríguez's career turned around—and real success resulted—when he toured with the Senior PGA. In his second season, in 1987, he set a record by winning seven tournaments. In just two years, he matched his lifetime earnings. By 1993 he had won 21 tournaments on the PGA Senior Tour. His earnings have now rocketed past the three-million-dollar mark.

On the course, Rodríguez's trademark is a white Panama hat and a crowd-pleasing matador act. After sinking a putt, he waves his golf club like a sword, stabs an invisible bull, wipes off the imaginary blood, then slides it into a make-believe scabbard at his side. He trades jokes with spectators, signs autographs, and poses for photographs.

Devotes Life to Helping Children

Rodríguez still loves golf, but his real passion is working with the Chi Chi Rodríguez Youth Foundation in Florida. The foundation helps disadvantaged and troubled kids, ages five to fifteen. The kids receive free counseling and tutoring, and they participate in sporting activities. Rodríguez started the foundation in 1979 after he visited a Florida detention center and wanted to do something to help the young inmates. "Seeing those kids trapped like animals inside cells broke my heart," he told Sue Cronkite in *Life*.

Since the foundation's beginning, hundreds of children have benefitted from its training. The governments of Nepal and Costa Rico have expressed an interest in expanding the Chi Chi Rodríguez Foundation to their countries. For his work, Rodríguez is lauded everywhere he goes. In 1986 he became the first athlete to receive the prestigious Horatio Alger Award for humanitarianism. Although Rodríguez is flattered by the praise he receives, his rewards for the work he does with the foundation come directly from the children. "I just feel like I'm in heaven," he told Tim Rosaforte of *Business Week*, "the peace of God comes over me, when these kids touch me on the shoulder and say, 'Uncle Chi Chi.'"

For Further Information

Business Week, February 10, 1992, pp. 53-58; February 8, 1993, pp. 71-77.
Life, August 1989, pp. 48-61.
New Choices, June 1989, pp. 40-46.
Saturday Evening Post, March 1989, pp. 52-53.

Paul Rodríguez

Comedian
Born c. 1955, Mazatlán, Mexico

"Comedy was my secret weapon. It saved my life many times. I wasn't the meanest dude in the barrio, but I was the funniest."

Paul Rodríguez is one of the most recognized Hispanic comedians in the United States. His face first became familiar to Americans in the mid-1980s through comedy specials on cable television and comedy series on network television. On the surface, much of his humor seems to make fun of Hispanics. Upon deeper examination, his humor exposes the limited, stereotypical view many Americans have of Hispanics and Hispanic life.

Rodríguez was born around 1955 in the Pacific seaport town of Mazatlán in the Mexican state of Sinaloa. With little money, his family immigrated to the United States when he was just a child. They settled in a rough East Los Angeles barrio (Spanish-speaking neighborhood). Rodríguez recalled his childhood to a reporter in *People:* "Comedy was my secret weapon. It saved my life many times. I wasn't the meanest dude in the barrio, but I was the funniest."

Members of his family struggled to make a living as migrant farm workers. Although the rights of farm workers were improving slightly in the 1960s (see **César Chávez** and **Dolores Huerta**), the working conditions they faced were still harsh. Even so, Rodríguez's parents were happy to have any job

Paul Rodríguez

California State University with plans to become a lawyer. During theater classes at the university, Rodríguez's comic talent so impressed his professor that he took Rodríguez to amateur night at the Comedy Store nightclub. Rodríguez's career was launched. He dropped out of school and began performing at colleges and at Spanish and English clubs throughout Los Angeles.

Rodríguez's sharp-edged humor soon caught the attention of television producers. In 1984 he was cast as the lead in *a.k.a. Pablo,* a situation comedy developed by Norman Lear that aired on ABC. The show centered on Rodríguez's character, but also focused on his Hispanic family and their daily routines. The show was canceled, however, after only six episodes aired. Many Hispanic groups objected to Rodríguez's jokes, which they found offensive to Mexicans and Hispanics in general.

The criticism did not stop Rodríguez from continuing his act. To this day, he is unfazed by what other people think of him. "I never read reviews written about me," he explained to Jane Marion in *TV Guide,* "because in reality I'm never as good as they say I am, and I'm never as bad as they say I am. I know who I am."

to support their family. They disapproved of their son's childhood fantasies. "My family never thought that being a comedian or an actor was an obtainable goal," he said in *Hispanic American Almanac.* "Being farmworkers, all they wanted for their children was a steady job. But I knew I had to give it a chance."

From the Air Force to Comedy Clubs

In 1977 Rodríguez enlisted in the U.S. Air Force and served as a communications specialist. During his four-year stint, he lived in 33 countries around the world, including Iceland. After his discharge, he entered Long Beach City College and earned an associate arts degree. He then enrolled in

Wins Parts in Motion Pictures

Rodríguez found 1986 to be a busy year. He played supporting roles in three motion pictures: *Miracles, Quicksilver,* and *The Whoopee Boys.* Of the three, *Quicksilver* had the greatest box-office appeal. The movie starred Kevin Bacon as a young stockbroker who loses everything, then becomes a city bicycle messenger. That same year, Rodríguez also released his first comedy album, *You're in America Now, Speak Spanish.*

Rodríguez was given a second chance at a television series in 1988. CBS offered him the chance to play in the situation comedy *Trial and Error.* Rodríguez portrayed the character of Tony, a T-shirt salesman. He rooms with John (played by Eddie Vélez), a newly graduated Puerto Rican lawyer working in an established law firm. Although the show was also broadcast in Spanish on Spanish-language radio stations, it never attracted a sizable audience and was canceled.

Rodríguez's media ventures since then include his stint as host of the syndicated television show *The Newlywed Game* and his performance in the highly acclaimed HBO comedy special "I Need a Couch." He has continued to lend his talents to various motion pictures. In 1993 he played a supporting role in the comedy *Made in America,* which starred Whoopi Goldberg and Ted Danson. Rodríguez made his directorial debut in 1994 with *A Million to Juan,* a modern-day adaptation of American writer Mark Twain's story "The Million-Pound Bank Note."

Performs Benefits for the Disadvantaged

Rodríguez is the head of his own company, Paul Rodríguez Productions. In 1991 his company produced the one-hour special "Paul Rodriguez behind Bars," which aired nationally on the Fox Network. The show highlighted Rodríguez performing for prison inmates. Throughout his career, he has performed for the poor and disadvantaged. In 1992 he helped singer Gloria Estefan (see **Gloria Estefan**) raise money to help the Florida victims of Hurricane Andrew. The benefit performance also included Whoopi Goldberg, Paul Simon, Rosie O'Donnell, and Andy García (see **Andy García**).

In addition to performing stand-up comedy in Las Vegas and Atlantic City, Rodríguez hosts and stars in the popular *El Show de Paul Rodríguez* on Univision, the Spanish-language television network. He also appears as a Spanish-language spokesman for Miller Brewing Company, GTE Corporation, and Highland Superstores. Rodríguez is happy to reach out to his community, but he feels advertisers are allowing him to reach out only to a part of it. "I'm very proud of being Mexican American," he explained to Ruth Stroud in *Advertising Age,* "but I'm not just Mexican American—I'm American."

For Further Information

Advertising Age, October 16, 1989.
Hispanic, June 1994, p. 14.
Hispanic-American Almanac, Gale Research, 1993.
People, June 27, 1983, p. 96.
TV Guide, July 1, 1989, p. 19.

Richard Rodríguez

Writer, journalist
Born July 31, 1944, Sacramento, California

"We come from an expansive, an intimate, culture that has long been judged second-rate by the U.S. Out of pride as much as affection, we are reluctant to give up our past."

ichard Rodríguez could not speak English when he began elementary school in California. As the son of Mexican American immigrants, he had grown up speaking nothing but Spanish at home. Still, he was quite successful in school, eventually earning degrees from several universities. Today he is a controversial social critic of bilingual education and affirmative action programs. He urges Hispanics in the nation not to think of themselves as foreigners but to consider themselves full Americans.

Rodríguez was born in 1944 in Sacramento, California, to parents who had immigrated to the United States from Mexico only a few years before. The Irish Catholic nuns at Rodríguez's school encouraged his parents to use English at home to help their children's performance in school. Rodríguez's parents agreed, wanting their children to blend into American society, despite the odds against it. But Rodríguez regrets the loss of closeness that his family felt before they gave up that piece of their private culture. Throughout much of his adult life, he has struggled with the desire to recapture that private culture, while holding on to gains earned in the mainstream American culture.

Rodríguez reached the goals his parents wanted for him. He was an outstanding student throughout his academic career. After high school, he attended Stanford University, earning his bachelor of arts degree in English in 1967. Two years later he earned a master of arts degree in philosophy from Columbia University. He then worked toward a doctorate in English at the University of California at Berkeley for several years. During his doctoral work, he studied for a year in England.

Although Rodríguez achieved academic success, he eventually began to fight against the very policies that helped him achieve that success. Throughout his college years he received financial help partly because he was an ethnic minority. Later, he turned down teaching jobs that were offered to him as part of affirmative action programs (government policies designed to help minorities achieve equal status in the workplace). He found it ironic that the job offers were based on his identity as a "minority," when his achievements were based on his struggle to blend in with the "majority."

Instead, Rodríguez decided to become a journalist and writer. He began working with the Pacific News Service in San Francisco, eventually becoming an editor. His articles for the service have been picked up for publication by newspapers all over the country. Rodríguez has written for national newspapers such as the *Los Angeles Times* and for national magazines such as *Harper's*. He has also worked as a journalist and essayist for public television's *MacNeil/Lehrer News Hour.*

Many of Rodríguez's articles have focused on what it means for Mexicans to come to America and to assimilate (become absorbed) into its culture. Many Mexicans, and their Mexican American children, fear that they will lose their identity—their culture—if they become a part of the American mainstream. "We come from an expansive, an intimate, culture that has long been judged second-rate by the U.S.," Rodríguez wrote in an essay in *Time.* "Out of pride as much as affection, we are reluctant to give up our past."

Rodríguez goes on to argue, however, that this type of thinking is wrong. He believes that what has made Mexican culture (and all

Hispanic cultures) great is that it has grown through assimilation. The culture of Latin America, Rodríguez points out, clearly reflects the cultures of other nations—European and African—that have played a part in its history. The ability of Hispanics to interact and intermingle with other peoples is what defines them. "The remarkable legacy Hispanics carry from Latin America is not language—an inflatable skin—but breath itself, capacity of soul, an inclination to live," Rodríguez wrote in *Time.* "The genius of Latin America is the habit of synthesis. We assimilate."

Rodríguez's most intensely personal writings have been in two books—*Hunger of Memory: The Education of Richard Rodríguez* and *Days of Obligation: An Argument with My Mexican Father.* Rodríguez spent six years writing *Hunger of Memory,* published in 1983. The autobiographical work—composed of five essays—offers an intense and thoughtful look at his humble beginnings, his education, and at how language has played a part in his life. In the book, Rodríguez argues against the idea that minorities should be hired for jobs simply because they are minorities. He also does not believe in bilingual education. Rodríguez feels that it simply widens the sense of separateness Hispanic students already feel from mainstream America.

In 1992 Rodriguez published *Days of Obligation.* Like his previous book, *Days of Obligation* is a collection of essays. Through these writings, Rodríguez tries to understand the meaning of Mexico, his Mexican ancestors, the Mayans (Indian peoples chiefly of Yucatán, British Honduras, Guatemala, and the state of Tabasco, Mexico), and the Catholic religion from his father's viewpoint. In one essay, he explores the myth of Joaquín

Richard Rodríguez

Murieta (see **Joaquín Murieta**), the nineteenth-century California bandit. "In imaginatively exploring the life of such a myth," Ilan Stavans wrote in *Commonweal,* "Rodríguez comes to see the Rio Grande as a psychic injury dividing the idiosyncracies of Mexico and the United States."

Rodríguez's writings and ideas have earned him many awards. In November 1992 President George Bush presented him with a Charles Frankel humanitarian award. At the same time, his writings have deeply divided Mexican Americans. He is unfazed by the criticism. What is most important for him is to explore and close the gap that exists between the Mexican Rodríguez and the American Rodríguez.

For Further Information

Commonweal, March 26, 1993, pp. 20-22.
Nation, January 18, 1993, pp. 63-65.
National Catholic Reporter, November 20, 1992, p. 33.
Time, July 11, 1988, p. 84; January 25, 1993, pp. 69-70.

Linda Ronstadt

Singer, actress
Born July 15, 1946, Tucson, Arizona

"I loved the idea of doing a work particular to Mexico. La Pastorela is not found in Cuba or Venezuela. People tend to lump Hispanic cultures together."

Few performers today have been more daring in their work than Linda Ronstadt. She is a singer who has made her mark in such varied styles as rock, country, operetta, old-fashioned ballads, and mariachi (Mexican street band) music. Almost every musical experiment Ronstadt has undertaken has met with success, fan approval, and hefty record sales.

Ronstadt was born in 1946 in Tucson, Arizona, to Mexican American parents Gilbert and Rosemary Ronstadt. Her father used to sing on local radio stations around Tucson and had also appeared with big bands in the area. During the Great Depression (a period in the 1930s when the nation suffered from an extremely slow economy and widespread unemployment), he gave up singing to run a hardware store.

Ronstadt and her brothers and sister were constantly exposed to the Mexican music their father loved while they were growing up (she would later make an album of his favorite songs). Ronstadt enjoyed harmonizing with her siblings, and decided by the age of six to become a singer. She promptly lost all interest in school. By her teen years, she was well-known at Tucson's Catalina High School for her outstanding voice.

Ronstadt says she developed a habit of rebellion early in life. She stuck to her ideas with singleminded determination. She attended the University of Arizona briefly, dropping out at 18 to join her musician boyfriend in Los Angeles. With her boyfriend and another male musician, Ronstadt formed a folk-rock group called the Stone Poneys. The group's only hit was "Different Drum," a single from their second album, *Evergreen, Volume II,* released in 1967. An intense touring schedule, problems with drug abuse, and a series of disappointing concert appearances caused the Stone Poneys to break up after only a few years.

Solo Career

Ronstadt then began her solo career. By 1970 she had released two albums that fused country and rock styles: *Hand Sown ... Home Grown* and *Silk Purse.* The latter album produced her first solo hit, the sorrowful "Long, Long Time." Today this song is considered a classic ballad. In fact, actors have been known to listen to it to bring them to tears when they need to cry for sad scenes.

Ronstadt's voice seemed particularly suited to melancholy music. She has described her childhood as lonely and her early singing career as bleak. She was bothered by the stresses of constant touring, a difficult love life, and cocaine use. Music critics paid little attention to her work. To make matters worse, she suffered from stage fright.

In 1973 Ronstadt moved to a different recording company and hired a new producer and manager. The changes seemed to alter the direction of her life. The next year she recorded her first million-selling album, *Heart Like a Wheel.* By the mid-1970s, she had established herself as rock's most popular female star with hits such as "When Will I Be Loved?," "Desperado," "You're No Good," "Blue Bayou," and "Poor, Poor Pitiful Me."

Makes the Leap to Opera

The musical leap from rock to opera is gigantic; few voices can make it successfully. In 1981 Ronstadt astonished critics and fans by making that leap gracefully. She sang a difficult soprano role in the Broadway operetta, *The Pirates of Penzance.* Three years later, she performed the part of Mimi in Giacomo Puccini's nineteenth-century opera *La Bohème.*

In the mid-1980s Ronstadt pushed her abilities in an entirely different direction. She recorded three albums of sentimental American love songs from the 1920s and 1930s: *What's New?, Lush Life,* and *For Sentimental Reasons.* For these songs she chose to be backed by the vintage Nelson Riddle Orchestra. Her manager and friends tried to talk her out of the project, figuring that her fans would desert her and her record sales would plummet. Surprisingly, the albums were a great success. "Instead of trying to re-create another era's erotic climate," Stephen Holden wrote in *Vogue,* "[Ronstadt]

Linda Ronstadt

pays homage to it with lovely evenhanded line readings offered in a spirit of wistful nostalgia."

Reaches Back to Mexican Roots

Ronstadt followed up these successes with a switch to country. In 1986 she earned several awards for *Trio,* an album she recorded with country stars Dolly Parton and Emmylou Harris. In 1987 she went back to the songs of her childhood, releasing *Canciones de mi padre.* The album, her first in Spanish, featured mariachi songs that her father used to sing.

In 1989 Ronstadt returned to a mainstream sound with *Cry Like a Rainstorm—Howl Like a Wolf.* Several of the album's tracks featured Ronstadt singing with Aaron Neville. One of their duets, "Don't Know Much," went to the top of the charts.

In 1991 Ronstadt once again returned to her Mexican roots. She recorded *Mas canciones,* another album of traditional Mexican songs sung in Spanish. She also returned to the stage in *La Pastorela,* an updated version of the traditional Mexican folk play about the shepherds traveling to worship the infant Jesus. Directed by Luis Valdez (see **Luis Valdez**), the play aired on public television. "I loved the idea of doing a work particular to Mexico," she told Edna Gunderson in *TV Guide.* "*La Pastorela* is not found in Cuba or Venezuela. People tend to lump Hispanic cultures together."

Ronstadt's next two projects focused on the Afro-Cuban music that invaded America during the 1940s and 1950s. She took part in the soundtrack recording of the 1992 movie *The Mambo Kings.* The film was based on the Pulitzer Prize-winning novel by Oscar Hijuelos (see **Oscar Hijuelos**). On the soundtrack, Ronstadt sang a classic torch song (a popular sintimental song of unrequited love) from the time, "Perfidia." She explored that music even further in 1993 when she recorded *Frenesí,* an album composed entirely of songs from the 1940s and 1950s.

In 1994 Ronstadt continued to surprise the music world with her wide variety of talents. She offered *Winter Light,* her first pop album in four years. The record featured songs by such 1960s songwriters as Burt Bacharach, Carole King, and Brian Wilson of the Beach Boys. *People* magazine's Brian Carmody wrote that Ronstadt "is worth hearing, as always, and this new album only enhances her reputation as an accomplished interpreter of classic pop music."

For Further Information

Amdur, Melissa, *Linda Ronstadt,* Chelsea House, 1993.
Hispanic, October 1988, pp. 10-14.
People, January 17, 1994, p. 23.
Vogue, November 1984.
TV Guide, December 21, 1991.

Carlos Santana

Musician
Born July 20, 1947, Autlán de Navarro, Mexico

"I play music because I know it can elevate the spirit, because it has the power to build the bridge of love between people."

F ew performers have lasted as long in the world of rock music as Carlos Santana. He and his band made their breakthrough performance at the Woodstock rock festival held during the summer of 1969 near Bethel, New York. Since that time, many popular musical styles and musicians have appeared and disappeared. The lasting effect of Santana and his various ensembles is due to his music's universal appeal. His musical style combines elements of American blues and jazz, African rhythms, and Latin American salsa. "I play music because I know it can elevate the spirit," he told *Down Beat*'s Dan Ouellette, "because it has the power to build the bridge of love between people."

Santana comes from a family with a long history of musicianship. He was born in 1947 in Autlán de Navarro, west-central Mexico, to José and Josephina Santana. Both his paternal grandfather and great-grandfather were musicians. His father, a *mariachi* (Mexican street band) violinist, taught him to play both the violin and the guitar.

While he was still young, Santana and his family moved to the city of Tijuana, just across the Mexican-American border from San Diego, California. There he became influenced by American blues, listening to early recordings of guitarists B. B. King and T-Bone Walker. As he grew older, he began to play guitar in small nightclubs on the seamier side of Tijuana.

Influenced by Jazz and Salsa

In the early 1960s, Santana's family moved again, this time to San Francisco, California. Jazz was a popular musical style in this cosmopolitan city, and it quickly influenced Santana's playing. He was especially drawn to the musical style of saxophonist John Coltrane, and his musical tastes were expanded even further after he began listening to salsa musicians such as Tito Puente (see **Tito Puente**). *Salsa* (Spanish for "sauce") is a fiery Latin American dance music of Afro-Cuban origin.

Santana founded the band Santana in 1966 with bass guitarist David Brown and keyboardist Gregg Rolie. The band's sound—a combination of blues, jazz, rock, and Afro-Latin American rhythms—caught on quickly in U.S. cities. A large audience developed among Mexican, Puerto Rican, and Latin American listeners. Soon, music-lovers of all backgrounds were dancing to the band's rhythmic beat, a sound that came to be known as Latin rock.

The band Santana made its national debut at the three-day Woodstock festival in 1969.

Carlos Santana

Although the band was still a local, San Francisco-area phenomenon and had not yet recorded an album, they played alongside such rock veterans as Jimi Hendrix, Janis Joplin, and the Who. A documentary of the festival, *Woodstock,* was released in 1970, and many critics consider Santana's rousing performance to be the highlight of the film. It brought the band to a worldwide audience. People who previously had not listened to jazz or Latin music now sought out the group's first albums.

Spirituality Guides His Music

Santana (1969), *Abraxas* (1970), and *Santana III* (1972) all became best-selling albums with chart-topping singles like "Evil Ways," "Black Magic Woman" (recorded earlier by Fleetwood Mac), "Oye Como Va" (composed by Puente in the 1950s), and "Samba Pa Ti." In the early 1970s, Santana disbanded and reformed his group many times. He also performed with many other solo musicians, including John Coltrane and fellow guitarist John McLaughlin.

During this time Santana underwent a spiritual conversion to the teachings of Sri Chinmoy Ghose, an Indian mystic and poet. Sri Chinmoy emphasized the need to develop the heart over the mind and to celebrate God in all daily activities. Santana applied this teaching to his approach to music. As he told Jas Obrecht of *Guitar Player,* "Whether in a cry or in a party atmosphere, the music should exalt humanity and the spirit of humanity, which is the Lord." He also adopted the spiritual name "Devadip," which means "Eye of God."

Throughout the 1970s and 1980s, Santana switched between group and solo projects. The band continued to blend rock with salsa, and their 1981 release *Zebop!,* featuring the hit "Winning," was an especially big seller. Meanwhile, Santana used his solo work to express his deep religious feelings.

Uses Music to Benefit Social Causes

Santana has also conveyed his message of spiritual awareness through a variety of political and social benefits. In 1981 he appeared in concert with yet another lineup of his band to benefit United Cerebral Palsy. In 1985 they reformed to participate in Live Aid, the worldwide benefit concert for famine victims in Ethiopia. The following year Santana joined with rap artists Run-D.M.C. at a Crack-Down concert to raise awareness about the dangers of crack cocaine. And in 1988 he helped organize the "Blues for Salvador" benefit concert that raised $100,000 for the children of El Salvador.

"Musicians can be healers, more so than politicians, senators, presidents, or generals," Santana told Ouellette in *Down Beat.* In 1991 he and his wife, Deborah, opened their home in Marin County, California, to local schoolchildren to show them what the life of a musician is like. The tour was part of a program sponsored by the Cities in Schools (CIS) an organization formed to help improve the lives of underprivileged students. Deborah Santana is a member of the board of directors of CIS.

Almost 30 years after they began, Santana and his band continue to record and to tour the world. In late 1993 the band released *Sacred Fire: Santana Live in South America.* And in August of 1994, they took part in Woodstock '94, the 25th anniversary celebration of the original festival. For Santana, the point of his music has remained the same throughout the years. "What means something," he explained to Obrecht, "is to be able to tell a story and put wings in people's hearts."

For Further Information

Detroit Free Press, August 7, 1994, p. 4G.

Down Beat, August 1991, pp. 28-29; May 1992, p. 12.

Encyclopedia of Rock, edited by Phil Hardy and Dave Laing, Schirmer Books, 1988.

Guitar Player, January 1988, pp. 46-54.

Hispanic, October 1992, p. 80.

The Rolling Stone Encyclopedia of Rock & Roll, edited by John Pareles and Patricia Romanowski, Rolling Stone Press/Summit Books, 1983.

Stambler, Irwin, *The Encyclopedia of Pop, Rock & Soul,* revised edition, St. Martin's, 1989.

George Santayana

Philosopher, poet, novelist, critic
Born December 16, 1863, Madrid, Spain
Died September 26, 1952, Rome, Italy

*"Although he was born in Spain and edu-
cated in the United States, Santayana was
a true citizen of the world."*

George Santayana is recognized as one of the greatest philosophers of the twentieth century. He earned praise for his thoughtful, poetic writings and is credited with developing a universally appealing system of thought. While a young man, Santayana was a respected philosophy instructor at Harvard University. However, being a man of wide interests, he was not content to remain a teacher. Beyond thinking and writing, his main goal was to travel the world, and he spent the last 40 years of his life realizing that goal. Although he was born in Spain and educated in the United States, Santayana was a true citizen of the world.

Santayana was born in 1863 in Madrid, Spain, to Augustín Ruiz de Santayana and Josephine Borras Sturgis. His parents had come from separate regions in Spain and the differences in their cultural upbringings were difficult to overcome. In an effort to ease their marital tensions, they decided to separate for a while in the late 1860s. When Santayana was about six years old, his mother and her children from her first marriage sailed to America to live in Boston, Massachusetts. Santayana and his father remained in Spain in the small town of Avila.

Over the next few years, father and son grew close and forged a bond that would last for the rest of their lives.

Santayana was a gifted child who developed a love for language, literature, and the arts from his father. When they both finally sailed to the United States in 1872, however, young Santayana was at a loss: he spoke no English. At the age of nine, he was placed in a kindergarten class with children who were half his age. But with the help of one of his half sisters, Susana, he quickly learned to speak almost fluent English, and by 1874 he was enrolled in the prestigious Boston Latin School. There he studied mathematics, public speaking, English, French, Greek, and Latin.

Drawn to Architecture

Santayana's parents were not able to reconcile their differences, and in 1873 his father returned to Spain alone. Although Santayana loved his mother and half brothers and sisters, he was always closest to his father and was saddened by their separation. As a result, young Santayana withdrew socially, keeping mostly to himself and finding fulfillment in his studies. During this time, he became enchanted with architecture and read through all the books on the subject he could find. He made detailed drawings of buildings he saw around Boston and was soon creating original designs of palaces, cathedrals, and other buildings he imagined. Architecture remained an abiding interest.

While growing up, Santayana's greatest love was literature, especially poetry. In his last years at the Boston Latin School, he served as editor of the school paper and won prizes for his poetry. After his graduation in

George Santayana

1882, he was accepted into Harvard University. During his time there, Santayana blossomed. He made many friends, was involved in several clubs, and took part in many social activities, including university theater productions. Santayana's academic major was philosophy, and he was greatly influenced in his studies by one of his Harvard instructors, renowned philosopher William James. James exposed Santayana to empiricism, the philosophical belief that all knowledge comes from experience and that people develop ideas after they have received information through their five senses.

Santayana longed for a life of travel and learning, so after graduating from Harvard with highest honors in 1886, he sailed back to Europe. He continued his studies in Germany and traveled throughout other countries, viewing the architecture of ancient cathedrals. While in Europe, he developed the foundation for his future philosophic views. His ideas stemmed from the scientifically based theory of naturalism, the belief that everything that happens in the world comes from natural, not supernatural, causes. For Santayana, the forces that controlled man were the same ones that controlled nature. He believed man was secondary to the natural world around him.

Begins Teaching Philosophy

Santayana returned to Harvard in 1887 and completed his doctoral studies there two years later. He then planned to attend the Massachusetts Institute of Technology to study architecture, but William James convinced him to take over one of his classes at Harvard. Santayana agreed and his teaching career began. For the next 23 years, he lectured on philosophy to an increasing number of students, taking time off only to travel and to write. Among his students were future poets T. S. Eliot, Robert Frost, Wallace Stevens, and other bright young people who went on to make great contributions to the fields of journalism, history, and law.

Santayana maintained a keen interest in art, architecture, and poetry, and in 1894 he published his first book, *Sonnets and Other Verses*. More than anything he wanted to be a poet, but most reviewers criticized his efforts. Two years later, however, Santayana won over the critics when he published a book on aesthetics (the study of the philosophy of art and beauty) called *The Sense of Beauty.*

Santayana's position in the field of philosophy was further strengthened by his multivolume work *The Life of Reason,* which was published in 1905 and 1906. This five-book series explores the ways in which common sense, society, religion, art, and science contribute to contentment in a life led by reason. Santayana was again praised for his work, and Harvard made him a full professor. Over the next few years, he published works in areas ranging from philosophy to literary criticism. Despite the success and recognition these books earned, however, Santayana was not satisfied. Instead of teaching, he wanted to see the world and to write about his experiences and ideas. In 1912 he was given the chance to pursue his dream.

Pursues His Interest in Travel

That year Santayana's mother died, leaving him a small inheritance. He was a frugal man who managed his funds carefully; the money was more than enough to allow him to leave his position at Harvard and to spend the rest of his life traveling, studying, and writing.

For Santayana, travel meant a chance to experience new lands and new customs, which in turn increased his wide range of knowledge. Travel also fostered his sense of independence. Although he kept his Spanish citizenship and followed political events in his homeland, Santayana refused to settle down there. He did, however, frequently visit his father and his sister, who had moved back to Spain years earlier.

In 1927 Santayana published what many critics consider to be one of his most important philosophical works, *Skepticism and Animal Faith.* In this book, he departs from some of his earlier philosophical ideas. He sets out to show that people cannot always trust their senses to understand the natural world around them. Furthermore, he proposes that humans are able to function because of their natural "animal faith" (common sense), which allows them to interpret the world and lead meaningful lives.

Santayana believed that life can be divided into two realms—existence and essence. The realm of existence is made up of people, places, and other natural objects. The realm of essence is made up of ideas, colors, smells, and other things people come to know through their senses. Essences are thought to help people describe and understand existence. Santayana expanded on this idea in *The Realms of Being,* a four-volume work he published between 1927 and 1940.

Writes a Best-selling Novel

Throughout the late 1920s and the 1930s, Santayana continued to write other works, both philosophical and literary. In 1936 he published a novel titled *The Last Puritan.* The book, which focuses on a man whose actions in life are determined by his sense of duty, became a best-seller and was translated into seven languages.

After finishing the last volume of *The Realms of Being,* Santayana ended his traveling days, settling down in Rome, Italy, in 1941. He retired to a convent called the Clinica della Piccola Compagna di Maria, which was better known as the Home of the

Blue Nuns because of the color of the habits the nuns wore. While living at the convent, he completed work on his autobiography, *Persons and Places.*

Santayana spent his final years reading books from the convent's library, receiving admirers from around the world, and writing on subjects from politics to history. Shortly before his death, he began work on a book about the ancient Greek conqueror Alexander the Great. On September 26, 1952, Santayana died of stomach cancer. He was buried in Rome.

For Further Information

Arnett, W. E., *Santayana and the Sense of Beauty,* Peter Smith, 1984.

Carter, David, *George Santayana,* Chelsea House, 1992.

McCormick, John, *George Santayana: A Biography,* Paragon House, 1988.

Santayana, George, *The Last Puritan: A Memoir in the Form of a Novel,* Scribner's, 1936.

Santayana, George, *Persons and Places,* edited by William G. Holzberger and Herman J. Saatkamp, Jr., with an introduction by Richard C. Lyon, MIT Press, 1988.

Cristina Saralegui

Television talk show host, editor
Born January 29, 1948, Havana, Cuba

"I'm going to continue trying to help Hispanics cope with the problems brought on by modern living. If that's wrong, then sue me."

With her Spanish-language talk show, Cristina Saralegui is Hispanic television's answer to Oprah Winfrey. The writer and talk show host is not afraid to face controversy and insists her only goal is to inform Hispanics. Some critics say her topics are immoral and her blonde appearance un-Latin, but thousands of fans continue to tune in, giving her show a top ranking.

Cristina Maria Saralegui was born in 1948 in Havana, Cuba, to Francisco and Cristina Saralegui. Her grandfather, Don Francisco Saralegui, was a successful magazine publisher in Cuba. He was also the dominant influence in her early life. When she was a child, he would often take her to see his company's huge printing presses and editorial offices.

In 1960, shortly after Fidel Castro seized power in Cuba and installed a Communist government, Saralegui and her family left their comfortable life in Havana. They began anew in Miami's Cuban exile community. After attending high school, Saralegui prepared to enter her family's business by studying mass communications and creative writing at the University of Miami.

Initial Career in Journalism

In 1967 Saralegui obtained her first job, as an intern for *Vanidades Continentel,* Latin America's leading women's magazine. It was a huge challenge. Since she had attended high school and college in the United States, her English was better than her Spanish. She had to learn her original language all over again. She was successful enough to become features editor of the magazine by 1970. In 1976 she became the entertainment director for the *Miami Herald* newspaper. Three years later she was selected as the Editor-in-Chief of *Cosmopolitan-en-Español,* the Spanish-language version of *Cosmopolitan.* She held this position for ten years.

After 23 years as a journalist for Spanish-language magazines and newspapers, Saralegui moved into the television world in 1989. She became executive producer and host of *El show de Cristina* on Univision, the Spanish-language television network. The transition was not easy. She found that her personal appearance was an issue for the first time in her career. During her years as a writer, she spent most of her time behind a desk and never exercised. She had grown to a size 18.

Saralegui's good friends Emilio and Gloria Estefan sent her their personal fitness trainer. Determined to improve her health and looks, she rearranged her routine to include jogging three miles a day. She began watching her diet, changed her hair, and shrank six dress sizes.

Show Tackles Racy Issues

El show de Cristina became known for airing discussions on controversial topics,

Cristina Saralegui

such as sex. Many of the topics were previously considered "taboo" in the Spanish-language media. At first, Saralegui was worried that she'd have a hard time finding Hispanic guests willing to talk about personal issues. Once again, her appearance also became an issue. "People would write me hate letters," she told a reporter for the *Chicago Tribune.* "How dare I try to represent Hispanics when I was so white? I tried to make them see it was racism."

Despite the initially harsh criticism, Saralegui's show has been a huge success. It has been rated the number one daytime Spanish-language television show and ranked among the top ten Spanish-language programs in the United States. *El show de Cristina* won an Emmy award in 1991.

In 1991 the outspoken Saralegui also launched a three-minute daily radio show titled *Cristina opina* ("Cristina's Opinions"). The show gives her the chance to express her thoughts and concerns regarding Hispanic life. That same year she began another project, *Cristina la revista* ("Cristina the Magazine"). The monthly lifestyle magazine is an offshoot of her television program.

Emphasizes Hispanic Success Stories

By 1992 Saralegui had achieved another professional goal. She had become producer and host of *Cristina,* the English-language version of her Spanish talk show. She was the first Hispanic to host daily television programs in two languages. She has also produced a series of TV specials celebrating the lives of leading Hispanic entertainers. The point behind the specials is motivational. Many of the Hispanic celebrities profiled came from very poor backgrounds. Through hard work and dedication, they achieved success.

El show de Cristina continues to tackle sensitive issues, such as AIDS (Acquired Immune Deficiency Syndrome), rape, and incest. The five-year-old program, which airs in over 15 countries, continues to receive criticism. Through it all, Saralegui remains firm in her convictions. "I'm going to continue trying to help Hispanics cope with the problems brought on by modern living," she explained to S. Lynne Walker of the *San Diego Union-Tribune.* "If that's wrong, then sue me."

Saralegui is managed by her second husband, Marcos Avila (Avila is one of the founders of the music group Miami Sound Machine). She has two daughters and a son, and lives in Miami. She has won numerous awards, including being listed as one of *Hispanic Business* magazine's "100 Most Influential Hispanics" in 1992. Saralegui has also been named one of the "Legendary Women of Miami" and has received the Corporate Leader Award from the National Network of Hispanic Women.

For Further Information

Chicago Tribune, May 31, 1992.
Hispanic, November 1991, pp. 18-24.
Más, July/August 1991, pp. 43-50.
San Diego Union-Tribune, April 27, 1993. p. E1.

Junípero Serra

Franciscan missionary
Born November 24, 1713, Petra, Majorca
Died August 28, 1784, San Carlos de Carmel mission, California

"For good or for bad, Junípero Serra's mark on the history of the American West is undeniable."

The life of Junípero Serra, an eighteenth-century Spanish Franciscan missionary in North America, remains controversial to this day. Some view him as a pioneer who helped found settlements in California that grew into important cites such as San Diego and San Francisco and who brought Christianity to the native peoples of present-day California. Others claim he was a ruthless man who took over the natives' land and helped destroy their rich culture. For good or for bad, Junípero Serra's mark on the history of the American West is undeniable.

Serra was born Miguel José Serra in 1713 on Majorca, an island in the Mediterranean Sea off the eastern coast of Spain. His parents, Antonio and Margarita Serra, were peasant farmers, and Serra spent most of his childhood helping them in the fields around their village.

When not working in the fields, Serra spent his time in a Franciscan convent near his home. The Franciscans are a Roman Catholic order formed by Francis of Assisi in Italy early in the thirteenth century. They live under strict vows of poverty and prayer. The Franciscan friars at the convent quickly recognized the young Serra's intelligence and taught him reading, writing, Latin, mathematics, and theology. By the time he was sixteen, Serra had decided to become a Franciscan and entered the convent in the nearby capital of Palma. In 1731 Serra became a full member of the order and took the religious name of Junípero, who had been a companion of Francis of Assisi and who was known for his compassion.

Feels Call to Missionary Work

Serra then studied for three more years to become an ordained priest and a professor of philosophy. Even after he was already admired as a distinguished preacher and teacher, Serra continued with his studies, earning his doctorate in theology in 1742. He then traveled around Majorca, lecturing and preaching to the islanders. By 1749, however, Serra began to feel that his life would have greater meaning if he were a

Junípero Serra

missionary (a person who tries to convert others to his own religious beliefs). He soon left his position in Majorca and sailed to Mexico to spread his religious teachings to native Mexicans.

Mexico had come under the domination of Spain in the early 1500s when Spanish soldiers led by conquistadors (conquerors) like Hernán Cortéz destroyed the Aztec and other native tribes. Over the years, Spanish missionaries traveled throughout the area known as New Spain, setting up missions to convert the native people to Christianity and to European ways. When Serra arrived in Mexico City in 1750, the missions there were already well established.

Serra spent a year in Mexico City learning the native languages, then went to the Sierra Gorda region about 200 miles to the north to begin his mission work. Life at the missions was simple: in the morning, Serra conducted religious services for the Pame, the native inhabitants. Any Pame that missed services was given a lecture or even whipped. The Pame were forbidden to practice their own religious rituals and if they did, they were often whipped. During the day, the Pame tended the crops in the fields or helped build new stone churches or other structures. Serra stayed at the Sierra Gorda missions for eight years before returning to Mexico City to serve as a choirmaster and a supervisor of student priests.

Practices Extreme Self-Denial

During this period, Serra developed a reputation for learning and for self-denial. Late at night, he would often whip his own body until his flesh split and bled. He rarely slept or ate, devoting most of his time to prayer. He believed that if he caused his body pain and overcame his physical passions, his spirit would become stronger. Those around him thought he was a saint.

Because of his religious enthusiasm, Serra was chosen in 1768 to be president of the missions in present-day Baja California, the long, thin peninsula extending south from the present-day state of California. These missions were previously run by Jesuits, members of the religious order the Society of Jesus. The king of Spain, Charles III, had ordered them removed from the area in 1767 because he believed they were becoming too strong and might take over his throne. At first, Serra was eager to begin his new work. He soon discovered the missions had been ransacked by Spanish soldiers looking for gold and most of the native

people of the area had been killed off by European diseases like smallpox. Serra found he could change little in the area and became discouraged.

In 1769 José Gálvez, the visitor general of New Spain, asked Franciscan missionaries to colonize present-day California. This was done to prevent other explorers, such as the Englishman Francis Drake, from claiming the land that Spain believed it had already claimed. Serra believed he would be able to found a number of missions along the coast of California. In the spring of that year, Serra, a few other priests, and some Spanish soldiers began the march northward from Baja California.

Founds First Mission

Serra officially established his first mission, San Diego de Acalá, on July 16, 1769. It was the first permanent European settlement in present-day California. He worked hard trying to convert the natives of the region to Christianity, but he was unsuccessful at first. Raids by the natives almost wiped out the mission. A ship finally arrived in the spring of 1770 to resupply the mission, and Serra led a party northward to a site near the present-day city of Monterey. There he founded his second mission, San Carlos de Carmel. By the end of the year, Serra had begun to baptize the natives of California.

Over the next twelve years, Serra founded seven more missions, including one on the site of present-day San Francisco in October 1776. He died at the San Carlos mission on August 28, 1784, possibly from lung cancer. Missionary activity in California did not end with his death. His fellow Franciscans carried on his work, establishing another twelve missions by 1823 that helped to spur the growth of California. Many native people were baptized during the early days of these missions. Many more, however, were buried. In 1986 the Roman Catholic Church beatified Serra, which is the last step in the process to officially declare a person a saint.

For Further Information

Ainsworth, Katherine, and Edward C. Ainsworth, *In the Shade of the Juniper Tree,* Doubleday, 1970.

Dolan, Sean, *Junípero Serra,* Chelsea House, 1991.

Habig, Marion A., *Junípero Serra,* Franciscan Herald Press, 1987.

Moholy, Noel Francis, and Don DeNevi, *Junípero Serra: The Illustrated Story of the Franciscan Founder of California's Missions,* HarperCollins, 1985.

Charlie Sheen

Actor
Born September 3, 1965, New York, New York

"I didn't start out wanting to be an actor. I wanted to play baseball."

Charlie Sheen comes from a family of actors. His father, Martin Sheen, brothers Ramón and Emilio Estevez, and sister Renee Estevez have all followed careers in Hollywood. But Sheen wanted to branch out from the family business. "I didn't start out wanting to be an actor," he admitted to Elvis Mitchell in *Interview.* "I wanted to play baseball and had been offered a scholarship to play at the University of Kansas." When his baseball career fell through, however, Sheen joined his father and siblings in front of the camera. Since making that choice, he has gone on to become one of the busiest and most recognizable actors in Hollywood.

Sheen was born Carlos Irwin Estevez in New York City in 1965. (His father, Ramón Estevez, adopted "Martin Sheen" as his stage name in 1959). When Sheen was three years old, he moved with his family to Malibu, California. While growing up, he, his brother Emilio, and friends Christopher and Sean Penn spent their time acting in their own home movies. "When all the other kids were out surfing, smoking dope, and doing crazy things," he related to Todd Gold in *People,* "we were making super-8 [a type of film stock] movies."

Sheen often accompanied his father to movie sets. "I was always aware of what was going on technically [during film shoots]," he told Mitchell. When he was ten years old, Sheen spent eight months in the Philippines watching his father make *Apocalypse Now,* director Francis Ford Coppola's award-winning 1979 film about the Vietnam War. Sheen was present when his father suffered a near-fatal heart attack during the intense filming of the movie.

Tries for a Career in Baseball

To stand out in his family, Sheen turned his attention in high school from acting to baseball. "I thought, If I can excel at this, they'll think I'm something," he explained in an interview with Tom Green for *Cosmopolitan. "I'll* think I'm something." He went to a baseball camp in Missouri for four summers in a row. By the time he was a senior, Sheen was a star pitcher on his team and was given

Charlie Sheen

"I had a few scenes and I was eaten by a bear." Sheen quickly landed several other small roles, including parts in *Red Dawn* in 1984 and *Ferris Bueller's Day Off* in 1986.

Sheen's acting breakthrough came in 1986, when he played the lead character in Oliver Stone's Vietnam film, *Platoon*. Interestingly, when Sheen originally read for the part of the army recruit, Stone thought he was too young and chose his brother Emilio instead. Just before shooting was to begin, though, producers for the motion picture backed out. It took Stone a few years to gain the financial backing he needed to proceed with filming. This time, when Sheen re-read for the part, Stone thought he was perfect.

Platoon Brings Back Childhood Memories

Before filming on *Platoon* began, the cast had to participate in a two-week boot camp run by a retired Marine Corps captain. The camp and the filming, which took place in the Philippines, brought back a lot of memories for Sheen. Not all of them were pleasant. "I stepped off the plane and stopped," he recounted in the interview with Gold. "That smell hit me immediately: burning rubber, that poverty, that stench ... that's always in the air."

Like his father in *Apocalypse Now,* Sheen got caught up in the intensity of making a war film. After he returned home, it took him a while to readjust, as he explained to Mitchell: "I was depressed for about a month after I got back. I was just walking around, lost in space. Because everything had been so exciting."

Sheen followed up *Platoon* with a role in another hit film directed by Stone, *Wall Street.* In this 1987 movie, Sheen portrayed

a chance to attend college on a baseball scholarship. His performance in the classroom, however, did not match that on the field. Having attended only about a third of his classes, he was not allowed to graduate from high school and his college scholarship was taken away.

After leaving high school without a diploma, Sheen decided to give acting a try. Since his brother Emilio had already begun his acting career under the family name Estevez, Sheen adopted his father's stage name. His first role was in the 1984 horror movie *Grizzly 2: The Predator.* His small part in the low-budget film gained little notice. "I played a camper," he told Mitchell.

a young stockbroker who is seduced into breaking the law by a greedy businessman, played by Michael Douglas. Martin Sheen also made an appearance in the film, playing Charlie's working-class father.

Sheen's performances in *Platoon* and *Wall Street* quickly led to other roles. In 1988 he starred in *Eight Men Out,* about members of the Chicago White Sox who plotted to fix the 1919 World Series. He also worked on *Young Guns,* a western that revolves around Billy the Kid and his gang. Among the other young actors in this film were Emilio Estevez, Kiefer Sutherland, and Lou Diamond Phillips.

Stars in Film After Film

Since that time, Sheen has become one of Hollywood's busiest actors, starring in one to three films a year. In 1989 he made the baseball comedy, *Major League,* in which he played a sorry major league team's ace pitcher, known as Wild Thing. (He reprised his role in *Major League II,* released in 1994.) In 1990 he appeared on screen in three different movies: the action/adventure *Navy SEALS,* a police drama titled *The Rookie,* and the comedy *Men at Work.* Emilio Estevez wrote, directed, and also starred in this last film, about garbage collectors who get caught up in a murder.

In 1991 Sheen played one of his most popular roles, ace fighter pilot Sean "Topper" Harley in *Hot Shots!* The comedy, which was produced by the makers of the *Naked Gun* series of films, pokes fun at Navy flier movies such as *Top Gun* and at other popular hits like *Dances with Wolves.* In the 1993 sequel, *Hot Shots! Part Deux,* Sheen's character, Harley, is sent by the president of the United States to take on Iraqi president Saddam Hussein. Later in 1993, Sheen played one of the swashbuckling swordsmen in *The Three Musketeers,* based on the classic adventure tale by nineteenth-century French novelist Alexandre Dumas.

Quick success at a young age almost proved to be too much for Sheen. He told Laurence Gonzales in *Playboy* that he remembers very little about filming *Eight Men Out:* "I was taking too many drugs and drinking too much at the time." Now, Sheen approaches his acting roles more seriously, having realized that drinking and drugs limit his abilities. "You can't explore your options, and that's a lot of what acting is about," he told Mitchell. "I learned that from my dad."

Sheen received a star on the Hollywood Walk of Fame in September of 1994. That same month, his newly released action movie *Terminal Velocity* reached the Top Five at the box office.

For Further Information

Cosmopolitan, December 1987, pp. 102-08.
Interview, February 1987, pp. 35-40.
People, March 9, 1987, pp. 48-56.
Playboy, September 1990, pp. 116-18+.

Gary Soto

Poet, writer
Born April 12, 1952, Fresno, California

"We—Mexican Americans—need to have our stories told by books and movies—to see ourselves doing something."

Gary Soto began his career as an award-winning poet in the mid-1970s. By the early 1990s he had become a highly acclaimed writer of short stories and novels for young adults. In his entire collection of work, he has brought the sights and sounds of his barrio—the Spanish-speaking neighborhood where he was raised—vividly to life for all readers.

Soto was born in 1952 in Fresno, California, the center of the agricultural San Joaquin Valley. His parents, Manuel Soto and Angie Trevino, worked with his grandparents in the surrounding fields, picking grapes, oranges, and cotton. During the winter, or when field work could not be found, they worked in factories or warehouses. When Soto was five, his family moved to a Mexican American community on the outskirts of Fresno. A short time later, his father died in a factory accident. Soto's mother and grandparents had to struggle to raise young Gary, his brother, and his sister.

"I don't think I had any literary aspirations when I was a kid," Soto told Jean W. Ross in an interview for *Contemporary Authors.* "In fact, we were pretty much an illiterate family. We didn't have books, and no one encouraged us to read." While growing up, Soto had to help support his family by working in car washes or in the fields. Even though he graduated from high school with poor grades, he decided it was better to attend college than to work in a factory for the rest of his life.

Changes Focus After Reading Book of Poems

Soto enrolled at Fresno City College and chose to major in geography simply because he liked maps. He then discovered *The New American Poetry,* a collection of poems edited by Donald Allen. After reading the poems in the book, he was eager to begin writing his own poetry. He transferred to California State University at Fresno and signed up for creative writing classes. One of his instructors there was noted poet Philip Levine.

In 1974 Soto graduated magna cum laude (the second-highest academic ranking available). The following year he married Carolyn Oda, the daughter of Japanese American farmers. By 1976 he had received his master's degree in creative writing from the University of California, Irvine. He then began teaching at the University of California, Berkeley, first as an associate professor and later as a senior lecturer in the English department.

Soto's career as a poet began while he was still in graduate school. His poems earned him the American Academy of Poets Prize and the *Discovery-The Nation* Award in 1975. Within two more years, he had written enough poems to publish his first collection, *The Elements of San Joaquin.* The simply crafted poems in the book paint a grim picture of Mexican American people living in the barrios of Soto's youth and working in the fields of the San Joaquin Valley. Poverty and violence resound throughout. Despite its depressing tone, though, the collection has an underlying sense of hope, and many critics praised its realistic depiction of life for the region's Mexican American laborers. *The Elements of San Joaquin* won several literary awards, including the Bess Hokin Prize from *Poetry* magazine.

Soto's second book of poems, *The Tale of Sunlight,* was published in 1978 by the

University of Pittsburgh Press. It, too, presents images of impoverished Mexican Americans as they struggle to survive under difficult living and working conditions. Whereas the poems in the first book are mainly autobiographical, many of the poems in this second collection offer impressions through the eyes of two characters: Molina, a young boy, and Manuel Zaragosa, a tavern owner. Soto continued to write poetry in the early 1980s, publishing three more collections by 1985.

That year, however, the writer changed his focus by penning *Living up the Street: Narrative Recollections,* a collection of 21 autobiographical short stories or vignettes. "I wanted to do something different," he explained to Ross, "and I'm glad I did. It was a testing ground to see if I could write prose. I didn't tire of poetry, but I wanted to move into a thicker forest." Critics noted Soto's skill in writing about the poverty and racism that surrounded the day-to-day life of his childhood. *Living up the Street* won the American Book Award for 1985. Soto followed up this book with two other prose works, *Small Faces* in 1986 and *Lesser Evils: Ten Quartets* in 1988.

Writes for Young Readers

In the early 1990s Soto began writing short stories and novels aimed specifically at younger readers. "Literature can make a difference to the marginal kid," he explained to Nancy Needham in *NEA Today,* remembering his own awakening when he first read poetry. *Baseball in April, and Other Stories,* published in 1990, is a collection of 11 short stories about everyday events in a modern-day Mexican American neighborhood. Each

Gary Soto

story focuses on a different young person as its subject. For example, Alfonso wants to transform himself from an awkward young man into an Aztec warrior in "Broken Chain," and in "La Bamba," Manuel impresses his classmates with his lip-sync/dance performance at a school talent show until a scratch in the record ruins his act.

Even though almost all of Soto's stories for young readers take place in ethnic neighborhoods, his characters face conflicts that are universal. One example is his 1991 novel, *Taking Sides.* It follows Lincoln Mendoza, an eighth-grade Mexican American student, as he moves to a new neighborhood. One of the best basketball players for his old junior high school, he decides to join the basketball team at his new school. When his new team has to play a game against his old team, Mendoza must decide where his loyalties lie.

Soto has also used poetry and film to reach a younger audience. Two poetry collections, *A Fox in My Hands* (1991) and *Neighborhood Odes* (1992), present everyday aspects of Mexican American life through vivid descriptions—selling oranges door to door, running through a sprinkler on a hot summer afternoon, reading about the ancient civilizations of the Inca and the Aztec in a local library. Soto has also produced 16 millimeter films based on two of his short stories: "The Pool Party" is a ten-minute short for young viewers, while "The Bike" is a half-hour family feature.

In 1993 Soto edited *Places of the Heart: New Chicano Fiction,* a collection of short stories by 15 Mexican American writers. Through these writings—and through his own contributions to Hispanic literature—Soto hopes all Americans can share in the voices and experiences of Mexican Americans. His main goal, though, is to give Mexican American children an understanding of their heritage and their place in society. As he told Needham, "We—Mexican Americans—need to have our stories told by books and movies—to see ourselves doing something."

For Further Information

America, July 25, 1992, pp. 39-40+.
Contemporary Authors, Volume 125, Gale, 1989, pp. 424-27.
NEA Today, November 1992, p. 9.

Hernando de Soto

Spanish explorer
Born c. 1500, Jerez de los Caballeros, Spain
Died May 21, 1542, near present-day Ferriday, Louisiana

"Although the de Soto expedition was a failure for Spain, it nevertheless was one of the most remarkable in the history of North America."

Hernando de Soto was a Spanish explorer whose life was shaped by his relentless quest for gold in the New World. He helped the Spanish general Francisco Pizzaro bring about the fall of the great Inca empire in South America. Hoping to find treasure, he and his army traveled throughout the southeastern United States, becoming the first Europeans to explore that part of the country. In the process, he befriended and then betrayed many Native American tribes. He and his fellow Spaniards were probably the first white men to cross the Mississippi River. Although the de Soto expedition was a failure for Spain, it nevertheless was one of the most remarkable in the history of North America.

De Soto was born around 1500 in the village of Jerez de los Caballeros in the Spanish province of Estremadura. He was a descendant of a noble family, but grew up with very little money. By the time he was 19 years old, he had become a soldier and was sent to America to become the lieutenant of Pedro Arias de Avila, the governor of Spanish-controlled Darien (part of present-day Panama). During the 1520s, de Soto's job was to explore areas northward, conquer the native peoples, and claim the country-side for Spain. He was successful.

In 1532 de Soto was sent to South America to help Pizarro lead the conquest of the area ruled by the Inca empire in present-day Peru. Together the two men traveled to the city of Cajamarca in the Andes Mountains to meet the Inca ruler Atahualpa. The day after the Spaniards arrived, Pizarro invited Atahualpa to dinner and then took him prisoner. The Inca revolted and Pizarro eventually killed Atahualpa. The following year, Pizarro, de Soto, and the Spanish army marched southeast to the Inca capital of Cuzco and quickly captured it, destroying the Inca empire forever.

Longs for Adventure

After staying in present-day Peru for a few years, de Soto returned to Spain. His share of the Incan treasures had made him a rich and famous man. He married Arias de Avila's daughter Isabel. Quickly bored with life at home, he longed to return to the adventure and the riches of the New World. King Charles V of Spain obligingly made him governor of Cuba and *adelantado* (captain-general) of Florida. As the *adelantado,* De Soto was to explore the entire region of the present-day southeastern United States, start settlements, and conquer and convert the native peoples in that area to Christianity. A more important task for de Soto, however, was to find gold.

Before he had left Spain, de Soto had heard stories of gold and vast riches in the wild, uncharted territory he now controlled. He left Spain in 1538 chasing the promise of

Hernando de Soto

these untold riches. After dropping off his wife in Cuba and gathering more supplies for his army of 600 men and 200 horses, de Soto sailed to the site of present-day Tampa Bay, Florida. He and his men landed on May 30, 1539.

When they found no gold in the area where they landed, de Soto and his men headed northward along the western coast. The explorers were pleased to find Florida had no mountains, knowing it would be easier to march on flat land. They were not pleased, though, to find swamps, mosquitos, insects, alligators, and snakes. They decided to set up winter camp in the area of present-day Tallahassee, Florida.

In the spring of 1540, the Spaniards headed northeast to look for gold and other valuables. Most of their searching proved worthless. In present-day Georgia, they gathered about 350 pounds of fresh-water pearls, but nothing else. They continued to explore.

Enslaves Native Americans

At first, the Indians welcomed and be-friended the Spanish visitors. The queen of one tribe even directed De Soto to the spot where he gathered the pearls. However, this trust extended by the Native Americans was not returned by the Spaniards. De Soto conquered, destroyed, and enslaved those he met. A favorite trick of his was similar to that of Pizarro: de Soto would invite a chief to visit, then hold him for ransom. After the ransom was paid by the tribe, the chief was often killed and his people were captured. The Spanish forced the Native Americans to provide them with supplies. They were more concerned with finding gold than spreading the teachings of Christianity.

Word soon spread from one tribe to another that the Spanish were not to be trusted. The Native Americans became less friendly, making travel more dangerous for de Soto's men. The different tribes tried to fight the Spanish soldiers, but their weapons and methods usually proved ineffective against the more advanced arms and strategies of the Spanish army. To rid themselves of the invaders, the Native Americans began to direct De Soto and his men farther north to find gold.

The Spaniards traveled through the present-day states of Georgia, South Carolina, and North Carolina, then crossed the Appalachian Mountains into Tennessee before heading south into Alabama. In the fall of 1540, near Mobil Bay in present-day Alabama, de Soto and his men engaged in a fierce battle with a group of Native Americans led by Chief Tuscaloosa. Three thousand Native American warriors were killed while 22 Spanish soldiers lost their lives.

After the battle, the Spaniards were forced to head to the northwest. They spent that winter in present-day northern Mississippi.

Follows Visions of Gold

On March 4, 1541, as they prepared to break their winter camp, de Soto and his men were attacked by native warriors. In the fight, 12 Spaniards perished. Running low on supplies and horses, the remaining Spaniards pushed on, heading northwest. In May they came upon the wide Mississippi River just south of present-day Memphis, Tennessee. They camped along its banks for a month, building barges in order to cross it. Once they reached the other side of the river, they continued their quest for treasure. The Native Americans in that area told de Soto stories of gold and silver, and he pushed his men westward through present-day Arkansas. The only treasures they found were buffalo hides.

Along the way, many soldiers were killed in fighting with Native Americans or died of hunger and illness. After spending the winter near present-day Camden, Arkansas, De Soto and his men worked their way south along the Mississippi River. Discouraged by his failure to find riches, de Soto fell ill, probably of malaria (a fever spread by mosquitos). On May 21, 1542, he died at the age of 42. So the Native Americans would not find De Soto's body, his soldiers weighted it with sand and cast it into the Mississippi River.

The riches de Soto had so desperately sought were never found. The remaining soldiers (about half of de Soto's original army) eventually made their way to Mexico and to Spain. The information they took back about the present-day southeastern United States later proved valuable to Europeans who colonized the area.

For Further Information

The Hispanic-American Almanac: A Reference Work on Hispanics in the United States, Gale Research, 1993, pp. 68-70.

Milanich, Jerald T., *Hernando De Soto and the Indians of Florida,* University Press of Florida, 1993.

Hudson, Joyce Rockwood, *Looking for De Soto: A Search through the South for the Spaniard's Trail,* University of Georgia Press, 1993.

Whitman, Sylvia, *Hernando De Soto and the Explorers of the American South,* Chelsea House, 1991.

Zadra, Dan, *De Soto: Explorer of the Southeast (1500-1542),* Creative Education, 1988.

Reies López Tijerina

Social activist
Born September 21, 1926, near Falls City, Texas

"Tijerina thought that present-day Hispanics would not be so poor if the land claimed by the original Spanish explorers had been passed down to them through the generations."

Reies López Tijerina is a fiery Mexican American activist who has urged Hispanics to stand up for their rights—even if it means fighting the United States government. His special cause was the recovery of land that he believed the United States had stolen from early Spanish settlers. He awakened many people to the plight of poor Mexican Americans. A controversial figure, Tijerina's methods were sometimes illegal.

Tijerina was born in 1926 in Texas, one of ten children of Antonio and Herlinda Tijerina. His father was a sharecropper (tenant farmer who gives a part of his crops to his landlord in place of rent). He grew up during the Great Depression, the period in the 1930s when the nation suffered from an extremely slow economy and widespread unemployment, and worked in his family's fields for most of his young life. When his family could not survive on the farm, they were forced into becoming migrant farm workers. Because of his family's frequent moves, Tijerina attended about 20 different country schools.

Starts Out as a Preacher

As a child, Tijerina was influenced by his mother's strong Christian beliefs. As he grew older, he became interested in Bible study. At the age of 18, he entered the Assembly of God Bible Institute in Ysleta, Texas. He left the school after three years, married Maria Escobar, then set off to become an itinerant preacher (one who travels from place to place).

In the mid-1950s, Tijerina and a group of migrant families bought some land in Arizona. They started a cooperative settlement named Valle de la Paz, which means Valley of Peace. They built houses and a church, and tried living together in harmony. The local white people were not pleased with the community, which they considered a gypsy camp. They called Tijerina and the others

Reies López Tijerina

communists. They harassed the group until the families were forced to leave.

Fights for La Tierra

Tijerina looked around and saw other Hispanics suffering. He began to believe that his people's troubles were directly related to having *la tierra* ("the land") stolen from them. Tijerina thought that present-day Hispanics would not be so poor if the land claimed by the original Spanish explorers had been passed down to them through the generations. He traveled to Mexico to study old documents about land rights. He discovered an old treaty that had been signed after the Mexican War. The war had broken out in 1846 between Mexico and the United States over land claims in the present-day southwest-ern United States. The Treaty of Guadalupe Hidalgo had promised protection for the land rights of Mexicans in that area of the United States.

In 1963 Tijerina helped to form an organization called the Alianza Federal de Mercedes (Federated Alliance of Land Grants). Its purpose was to represent the interests of Mexican Americans who wanted the U.S. government to return land they believed belonged to them. The group focused its efforts on land held by the U.S. Forest Service in New Mexico. In 1966 they staged a march on the state's capital where they presented their demands to the governor. They then tried to occupy and claim as their own an area of the Kit Carson National Forest. The government reacted by accusing Tijerina and the Alianza of vandalism. Fearing arrest, Tijerina disbanded the group. A few days later, however, he re-formed it as the Alianza Federal de Pueblos Libres (Federal Alliance of Free Towns).

Arrested and Jailed

In 1967 the Alianza had a violent confrontation with authorities at a New Mexico courthouse. A policeman and a jailer were wounded, and Tijerina was arrested. After many court trials and appeals, Tijerina was finally convicted for his part in the courthouse incident and sentenced to jail for one to ten years. In 1971, after spending more than a year in prison, he was released under the condition that he not hold office in the Alianza for five years.

For a time, Tijerina took a nonviolent, peacemaking stance in relations between Mexican Americans and the U.S. government. In 1976 he resumed presidency of the

Alianza and continued his peaceful approach. He attempted, without success, to interest Mexican presidents in the Treaty of Guadalupe Hidalgo and the land rights issue of Mexican Americans.

During the 1980s Tijerina lost much support for his cause when he grew confrontational once again. He began a campaign against Jewish people. He blamed them for the loss of land grants and for the present-day problems of Mexican Americans.

For Further Information

Bernard, Jacqueline, *Voices From the Southwest: Antonio José Martínez, Elfego Baca, Reies López Tijerina,* Scholastic Book Services, 1972.

Blawis, Patricia Bell, *Tijerina and the Land Grants: Mexican Americans in Struggle for Their Heritage,* International Publishers, 1971.

Cummings, Richard, *Grito! Reies Tijerina and the New Mexico Land Grant War of 1967,* Bobbs-Merrill, 1970.

Jenkinson, Michael, *Tijerina,* Paisano Press, 1968.

Lee Treviño

Professional golfer
Born December 1, 1939, Dallas, Texas

"If I proved anything, it's that you don't have to be born into the country club set."

When he was a young boy, Lee Treviño lived in a farmhouse located behind a golf course. Enchanted by the game but too poor to play it, he studied the forms of the golfers from his back yard. His studying paid off. Treviño went on to become a professional golfer, dominating the game in the early 1970s. When he retired from the Professional Golf Association (PGA) Tour in 1985, he had won thirty tournaments and had earned over three million dollars (the third highest total winnings in PGA history). As a member of the Senior PGA Tour, he continues to win tournaments and to delight fans with his easy charm.

Lee Buck Treviño was born in 1939 on the outskirts of Dallas, Texas. He was raised by his mother Juanita, a cleaning woman, and her Mexican father, a gravedigger. Their four-room farmhouse was located on the back of the Glen Lakes Country Club fairways. To help with the family finances, Treviño dropped out of school when he was 14 years old. He found work on the golf course as a greenskeeper and caddy.

When he was 17, Treviño enlisted in the U.S. Marine Corps. While stationed on the island of Okinawa in the Pacific Ocean south of Japan, he played golf for the Marine Corps. After his discharge in 1961, Treviño returned to Texas and found a job as golf pro at a small Dallas club. After practicing for five years, he entered professional tournaments in 1966. In 1968 he achieved his first major victory at the U.S. Open, where he also became the first player in history to shoot all four rounds of the event under par (accepted average score). Treviño was on his way to the top of the PGA Tour.

Best Player on the Tour

In 1970 Treviño was the leading money-winner on the tour. The following year was his best as a professional. He became the only golfer in history to win the U.S., British, and Canadian opens all in one year. Between April and July of 1971, he won five

Lee Treviño

tournaments. For these achievements, he was named PGA Player of the Year, Associated Press Male Athlete of the Year, and *Sports Illustrated* Sportsman of the Year.

With his extraordinary talents on the golf course, Treviño attracted a huge following of fans. They were also drawn to his light-hearted manner and his witty jokes on the course. In the middle of tournaments, Treviño has been known to stop to buy hot dogs and soda for the children in the surrounding galleries. Throughout his career, he has participated in benefit tournaments and has donated much of his earning to charities such as the March of Dimes and Multiple Sclerosis.

Struck by Lightening

After his superb play in 1971, Treviño went on to win the British Open in 1972 and the PGA Championship in 1974, among other tournaments. In 1975, however, Treviño and two other golfers were struck by lightning during a tournament near Chicago. Even though he underwent surgery to correct a herniated (ruptured) disc in his back, the injury seriously affected his game (he still suffers from back problems due to the accident). He went winless in 1976 and 1978.

In 1980 Treviño made a comeback by winning the Texas Open and the Memphis Classic. He was also awarded the Vardon Trophy for the fewest strokes per round (69.73 for 82 rounds), the fewest since golf great Sam Snead set the record in 1958. In 1981 he was elected to the World Golf Hall of Fame.

Treviño retired from the PGA tour in 1985. He became a golf commentator for NBC television, and conducted "Learn with Lee" golf clinics. His many product endorsements in commercials made him one of the most recognizable Hispanic faces in the United States, Mexico, Japan, and Latin America through Univision, the Spanish-language television network.

Dominates the Senior Tour

However, Treviño could not stay idle for long. In December 1989, when he turned 50, Treviño joined the Senior PGA Tour. In his rookie season on the tour, he won seven tournaments and earned over one million dollars, a Senior tour record. Over the next two years, he continued his winning ways.

An injury in June 1992 quickly put an end to Treviño's streak. He had already won five tournaments that year and was on his was to being named the Senior tour's Player of the Year (he eventually won the award). While hitting practice balls, Treviño tore a ligament in his left thumb. That December he underwent surgery.

By early 1994 Treviño had regained his winning form. In April he won the PGA Seniors Championship. It was his fourth major championship and his twentieth win in just four years on the Senior tour. Treviño continues to be an inspiration to those who watch the game from the galleries and from behind the fences. "If I proved anything," he was quoted as saying by Larry Cardenas in *Hispanic,* "it's that you don't have to be born into the country club set."

For Further Information

Gilbert, Thomas W., *Lee Treviño,* Chelsea House, 1992.

Hispanic, May 1988, pp. 34-39.

May, Julian, *Lee Treviño: The Golf Explosion,* Crestwood House, 1974.

Sports Illustrated, April 13, 1992, pp. 42-44; June 7, 1993, pp. 52-53; April 25, 1994, pp. 46-47.

Luis Valdez

Playwright, director, producer
Born June 26, 1940, Delano, California

"I have something to give. I can unlock some things about the American landscape."

Playwright and director Luis Valdez is considered the father of Mexican American theater. In 1965 he founded El Teatro Campesino, a theater of farm workers in California. This project inspired young Mexican American activists across the country to use the stage to give voice to the history, the myths, and the present-day political concerns of Mexican Americans. In later years, Valdez has tried to portray Mexican American life for a mainstream audience, and his popular 1987 film *La Bamba* helped him do that.

Valdez was born in 1940 in Delano, California, into a family of migrant farm workers. At the age of six he began to work in the fields with his parents and nine brothers and sisters. Because his family had to travel around California's San Fernando Valley following the ripening of the crops, his education was continuously interrupted. Despite this, Valdez managed to finish high school and to attend San Jose State College. He majored in English and explored his interest in theater. While in college he won a writing contest for his play, *The Theft.* Later, the college's drama department produced *The Shrunken Head of Pancho Villa,* his play about the problems facing a Mexican couple in America.

After graduating from college in 1964, Valdez joined the San Francisco Mime Troupe, but he couldn't give up telling stories and writing plays. During this time he learned the techniques of agitprop (agitation and propaganda) theater, in which a play puts forth political views and tries to spur the audience to act on those views.

For years migrant farm workers had to endure unhealthy working conditions. They worked long hours for extremely low wages and received no benefits. Finally, in 1965, migrant grape pickers in Delano decided to go on strike. These workers were backed by the labor leader César Chávez (see **César Chávez**) and the migrant worker union he helped found, the National Farm Workers Association.

Luis Valdez

Brings Theater to Farm Workers

Two months after the strike began, Valdez joined Chávez in his efforts to organize the farm workers of Delano. It was there that Valdez brought together farm workers and students to found El Teatro Campesino (the Workers' Theater). The original function of this group of actor-laborers was to raise funds and to publicize the farm-worker strike and the grape boycott. Their efforts soon turned into a full-blown theatrical movement that spread across the country capturing the imagination of artists and activists.

By 1967 Valdez and El Teatro Campesino left the vineyards and lettuce fields to create a theater for the Mexican American nation. The movement evolved into *teatro chicano,* an agitprop theater that blended traditional theatrical styles with Mexican humor, character types, folklore, and popular culture. All across America, Mexican American theatrical groups sprang up to stage Valdez's one-act plays, called actos. The actos explored modern issues facing Mexican Americans: the farm workers' struggle for unionization, the Vietnam War, the drive for bilingual education, the war against drug addiction and crime, and community control of parks and schools.

Hands Down Rules for Mexican American Theater

In 1971 Valdez published a collection of actos to be used by Mexican American community and student theater groups. He also supplied the groups with several theatrical and political principles. Included among these were the ideas that Mexican Americans must be seen as a nation with roots spreading back to the ancient Aztecs and that the focus of the theater groups should be the Mexican American people. Valdez's vision of a national theater that created art out of the folklore and social concerns of Mexican Americans was successful. The Mexican American theater movement reached its peak in 1976.

Valdez and others in the movement then tried to expand the Mexican American experience into areas that would reach all Americans. In 1978 Valdez broke into mainstream theater with a Los Angeles production of his popular play *Zoot Suit,* about

Mexican-American gang members during the Los Angeles race riots of 1942-43. The following year the play moved to the Broadway stage in New York. It was then made into a film in 1982, but this version failed to please both critics and audiences. Valdez was hurt by the experience. "It's painful to make a passionate statement about something and then have people ignore it," he explained to Susan Linfield in *American Film.*

La Bamba Brings Attention

Valdez remained determined to reach a national audience. His next play, *Corridos,* the dramatization of a series of Mexican folk ballads, was praised by theater critics. It was then made into a television production that aired on PBS in the fall of 1987. Valdez's breakthrough into mainstream America, however, had come earlier that summer. He had written and directed *La Bamba,* the screen biography of Ritchie Valens, the 1950s Mexican American rock-and-roll singer. Audiences across America learned not only about the tragically short life of Valens but also about the lifestyle and other elements of the Mexican American community. The movie was an overwhelming box office success.

"My work comes from the border," Valdez told Gerald C. Lubenow of *Newsweek.* "It is neither Mexican nor American. It's part of America, like Cajun music." Valdez has continued to write plays for the theater, for television, and for motion pictures that focus on the lives and the histories of Mexican Americans. In 1994 he began work on the script for a film about the life of César Chávez, who died in 1993. He has also remained artistic director for El Teatro Campesino. In the process, he believes he is simply exposing America to another part of itself. "I have something to give," he explained to Lubenow. "I can unlock some things about the American landscape."

For Further Information

American Film, July/August, 1987, p. 15.
Newsweek, May 4, 1987, p. 79.
New York, February 7, 1994, pp. 60-61.
New Yorker, August 10, 1987, pp. 70-73.

Ritchie Valens

Singer, guitarist, songwriter
Born May 13, 1941, Pacoima, California
Died February 3, 1959, Mason City, Iowa

"Ritchie Valens's story provided an opportunity for Americans to understand some of the problems and characteristics of the Chicano experience in America."

Ritchie Valens was one of the first Chicano (Mexican American) rock musicians to have a song reach the top 10 on the music charts in America. He moved ethnic music into the popular mainstream. He might have gone on to even greater achievements, but his life was cut short when he was killed in a tragic plane crash. He was 17 years old.

Valens was born Richard Valenzuela in 1941 in Pacoima, California. His heritage was Mexican Indian. He learned to play guitar at the age of nine and soon began to write his own songs. While a student at Pacoima High School, he formed a rock group called

Ritchie Valens

the Silhouettes. The band played at high school functions and at local dances.

When Valens was 17, he and his band were spotted by Bob Keene of Del-Fi Records in Los Angeles. Impressed with their sound, Keene offered the band a recording contract. In 1958 one of the group's first singles, "Come On, Let's Go," became a hit on radio stations in the western states. Valens and the Silhouettes were off to a good start.

Late in 1958 Valens made his motion picture debut, singing "Ooh My Head" in the teenage rock-and-roll film *Go, Johnny Go!* By December of that year Valens had scored another hit with a sweet, slow love song called "Donna," which he had written for his girlfriend. The flip side, "La Bamba," was an upbeat adaptation of a Latino folk dance. Both songs rocketed onto the record charts, and Valens's teenage fans multiplied rapidly.

Goes on Tour with Buddy Holly and the Big Bopper

Valens's face soon became known across America when he appeared on the popular Perry Como television show. He followed up with a tour of Hawaii. He then went on the road in the United States as part of a packaged rock tour featuring young stars Buddy Holly and the Big Bopper (J. P. Richardson).

The tour usually traveled by bus between concerts in different cities. Buddy Holly soon grew tired of the slow, cold, bumpy drives. He chartered a small plane to speed his group from Clear Lake, Iowa, to the next concert in Fargo, North Dakota. Richardson talked Holly's bassist (future country star Waylon Jennings) into giving up his seat.

Valens had never flown on a plane before and was eager to try. He flipped a coin with Tommy Allsup, Holly's guitarist, for the remaining seat on the plane. Valens won. Almost immediately after takeoff on the snowy February night, the plane crashed. Everyone aboard—Holly, Richardson, Valens, and the crew—were killed. Years later, singer Don McLean called it "the day the music died" in his classic song "American Pie."

La Bamba Retells Life

Valens's brief career might have faded from memory if not for the popularity of his few hit songs. Rhino Records reissued his recordings and a three-disc set, *The History of Ritchie Valens*. Then, in 1987, Columbia Pictures produced a successful film biography about Valens, *La Bamba*. The picture, written and directed by Luis Valdez (see **Luis Valdez**) was enormously popular. It starred Lou Diamond Philips as Valens, and the soundtrack featured Hispanic musicians Los Lobos (see **Los Lobos**) and Carlos Santana (see **Carlos Santana**).

La Bamba introduced Valens to another generation of teens. Hispanic viewers approved of its authentic language and setting. The film also touched on the problem of forming a Chicano identity in America, and on family rivalry and cooperation in the Chicano community. Years after his short life ended, Ritchie Valens's story provided an opportunity for Americans to understand some of the problems and characteristics of the Chicano experience in America.

For Further Information

Goldrosen, John, and John Beecher, *Remembering Buddy,* Penguin, 1987.

Mendheim, Beverly, *Ritchie Valens: The First Latino Rocker,* Bilingual Press, 1987.

U.S. News and World Report, August 10, 1987, pp. 48-49.

Francisco "Pancho" Villa

Mexican revolutionary and bandit
Born June 5, 1878, Río Grande, Durango, Mexico
Died July 20, 1923, Parral, Chihuahua, Mexico

"Villa carried with him the desires of the people of northern Mexico: to rule themselves freely and to improve their lives."

During the Mexican Revolution, fought between 1910 and 1920, Pancho Villa commanded the large Army of the North. He played a part in some of the most important events of that time. To some Mexicans, he was nothing more than a bandit who robbed and killed. But to others, he was a legend who represented hope in the fight for the good of the common people. Villa carried with him the desires of the people of northern Mexico: to rule themselves freely and to improve their lives. Even after the revolt ended, his legend grew and people honored his name in *corridos* (songs). Nearly 50 years later, Villa's name was placed on the walls of the Mexican Congress alongside the other heroes of the Revolution.

Villa was born Doroteo Arango on June 5, 1878, in the village of Río Grande in the northern Mexican state of Durango. His parents, Agustín Arango and Micaéla Arámbula, were sharecroppers (poor farmers who work land owned by someone else). Like his two brothers and two sisters, Doroteo probably received little formal schooling as a child. He spent much of his time doing odd jobs for his parents on the farm.

In 1893 Agustín Arango died and Doroteo, as the oldest son, became the man of the house. The following year, while he was working in the fields, Doroteo saw the owner of the estate harassing one of his sisters. He quickly ran to a cousin's house, picked up a pistol, then returned home and shot the owner three times, wounding him seriously. Immediately afterward, Doroteo escaped on a horse, a fugitive at the age of 16.

It was during his first year as a fugitive that he changed his name to Francisco Villa.

He stayed in the mountains near his home for the first few months, living off the land. Early in 1895 he was captured, but escaped after spending only a short time in jail. The local police made many attempts to capture Villa, but he constantly slipped out of their grasp. He did well as a bandit, seizing money and shipments from the mines in northern Mexico. With the money he stole, he helped his family and friends. At various times, he worked regular jobs—butcher, stonemason, miner. However, he had to leave these jobs and flee to the mountains when the police discovered his whereabouts.

During this period, Mexico was governed by an unjust president, Porfirio Diaz. Under his leadership, Mexico's social conditions worsened. Diaz favored the owners of the large farming estates, or haciendas. The common people had no voice in government; their land was taken from them and they sank deeper into poverty. By the early 1900s, even some wealthy landowners were unhappy with Diaz's strict and prejudiced government. In 1910 Francisco Madero, the son of a wealthy rancher from northern Mexico, called for a revolution to overthrow Diaz. Seeing his chance to fight for a fairer government, Villa joined the Mexican Revolution.

Over 300 men of all social ranks joined Villa: poor peasants, middle-class farmers, rich hacienda owners. In the beginning, Villa's army lacked horses and supplies. After taking what they could from wealthy Mexicans who supported Diaz, the Villistas (Villa's soldiers) began to win battles. In May 1911, Villa and his men captured Cuidad Juárez, a city on the Mexican-American border opposite El Paso, Texas. Since Cuidad Juárez was then the main entry point into Mexico from America, the Villistas controlled all the supplies coming into the country. Feeling helpless, Diaz resigned the presidency and sailed to Europe.

Arrested and Almost Executed

Madero then took over the presidency, and Villa continued to battle forces loyal to Diaz. General Victoriano Huerta, commander of Madero's government forces, did not like the fact that Villa did not follow orders and acted on his own. Late in May, Huerta had Villa arrested for disobedience and for robbing civilians. Villa would have been executed if Madero had not intervened to save him. Sent to a prison in the capital of Mexico City, Villa remained there until he escaped in late December. He made his way north to El Paso where he began to reorganize the Villistas.

In February 1913 Huerta betrayed Madero, had him assassinated, and then assumed the presidency. Villa immediately returned to Mexico to avenge Madero's death. He soon joined forces with those under Venustiano Carranza, the governor of the state of Coahuila. Over the next few months, Villa's band grew larger and larger, and its victories began to mount. On November 15 the Villistas intercepted a coal train headed into Cuidad Juárez and snuck aboard. When the train arrived in the city, Villa and his men jumped off, surprised Huerta's troops there, and captured the city in only a few hours.

By the beginning of 1914, Villa had an army totaling some 9,000 men. He continued to rob the villages and the areas he conquered, but he used the money collected to pay his men and to support the revolution. In June of that year he made his final attack

Francisco "Pancho" Villa

against Huerta, capturing Zacatecas, the capital of Coahuila. Huerta's forces were wiped out and he abandoned the presidency less than a month later.

Meets with Emiliano Zapata

After Carranza became the new Mexican president, his relationship with Villa began to fall apart. The two men disagreed over who should have control over certain areas in the country. By the autumn of that year, Villa had broken with Carranza and gathered the Villistas to fight against him. On December 4 Villa met with fellow revolutionary leader Emiliano Zapata (see **Emiliano Zapata** to coordinate their attack against Carranza.

The alliance between Villa and Zapata never worked. The two men had different ideas for the revolution and they could not unite against the strong forces of Carranza. In the spring of 1915, Alvaro Obregón, Carranza's leading general, began to destroy Villa's army. Within a three-month period, Villa lost over 15,000 men. By the end of summer, he no longer controlled a large army, but a small group of bandit revolutionaries.

Turns Against America

The American government, under President Woodrow Wilson, formally recognized the Carranza government in October 1915. This all but finished Villa as he could no longer obtain guns and supplies from across the border. In response, the Villistas became anti-American. In January 1916 they attacked a train near the city of Santa Isabel in the state of Chihuahua, killing 15 Americans aboard. In the early morning of March 9, Villa sent the Villistas to raid Columbus, New Mexico. Buildings were burned to the ground, and soldiers and civilians were slaughtered. General John J. Pershing then led an American force into Mexico in pursuit of Villa, but he gave up a year later when he realized he could not capture the Mexican revolutionary.

Villa's escape from Pershing earned him the respect of many Mexicans. Many more, however, no longer supported his cause. They were tired of the constant fighting and only wished for an end to the revolution. From 1917 to 1919, Villa led only minor, bandit-like raids. On May 20, 1920, Carranza was assassinated and his successor, Adolfo de la Huerta, quickly signed an agreement with Villa to end the revolt. The government gave a large hacienda to Villa and paid benefits to the widows and orphans of the Villistas. The Mexican Revolution came to an end.

Villa had made many enemies during his years as a revolutionary, and they sought their revenge in 1923. In the early morning of July 20, while driving his car through

Parral, Chihuahua, Villa was shot and killed by eight assassins. Three years later, robbers dug up his grave and stole his skull. Those criminals were never found.

For Further Information

Guzman, Martin Luis, *Memoirs of Pancho Villa,* University of Texas Press, 1965.

Machado, Manuel A., *Centaur of the North: Francisco Villa, the Mexican Revolution, and Northern Mexico,* Eakin Press, 1988.

O'Brien, Steven, *Pancho Villa: Mexican Revolutionary,* Chelsea House, 1994.

Rouverol, Jean, *Pancho Villa: A Biography,* Doubleday, 1972.

Raquel Welch

Actress
Born September 5, 1940, Chicago, Illinois

"I've always thought the older I get the more people would see that I have more to me than just my good looks."

The striking beauty that earned Raquel Welch international fame and fortune has sometimes been her enemy. She has won beauty contests and has been on countless magazine covers. She has starred on stage and in television specials, feature films, and fitness videos. Throughout, Welch has simply wanted to earn respect and recognition as a serious actress.

Welch was born Raquel Tejada in 1940 in Chicago, Illinois, the daughter of Armand Tejada, a Bolivian immigrant of Spanish heritage, and Josephine Hall, an American.

When Welch was two, her family moved to La Jolla, a beach town in southern California. In high school, Welch (known as "Rocky" to her friends) was very active. She was a cheerleader, a member of the drama club, and the vice president of her senior class. She also took ballet lessons. By the time she was 15, she had begun to enter and win beauty contests.

Welch graduated from high school in 1958, then took a job as weather girl with a local television station in San Diego, California. She also spent a year studying acting at San Diego State College. She married her high school sweetheart, James Westley Welch, in 1959. They had two children, Damon and Tahnee. After the couple divorced in 1964, Welch took her children to Hollywood, where she looked for work as an actress.

Achieves International Stardom

For a time, Welch's career went nowhere. Then she met and married Patrick Curtis, a public relations man. He started his own firm and spent most of his time managing her career. As a result, she finally became a star. Two movie roles were significant in vaulting Welch to stardom. In 1966 she played a serious scientist in a formfitting skin-diving suit in the award-winning film *Fantastic Voyage.* The following year, in *One Million Years B.C.,* she was cast as Loana Sthell, a mostly silent cavewoman who cavorts around in a fur bikini. This film was a tremendous success in Europe, and Welch appeared on 92 European magazine covers. Her status as a sex symbol was established.

Welch's sexy image was further enhanced in 1967 when she wore a daring costume to

Raquel Welch

the Academy awards ceremony. In the British comedy *Bedazzled,* she played the role of a deadly sin, Lillian Lust. Welch finished up the year by touring South Vietnam with comedian Bob Hope to entertain American soldiers stationed there during the Vietnam War.

Between 1968 and 1970, Welch was cast in many films that played up her sexy image. By the early 1970s, however, she began to chose roles that were viewed as controversial. In *Myra Breckenridge,* Welch played the man-like personality of the transsexual character Myron. Critics blasted the movie, which had been based on the novel by Gore Vidal.

Fired for Being "Difficult"

Rumors circulated through Hollywood that Welch was becoming a difficult actress to work with. She denied this. "All I ever fought for was quality in my films," she explained years later to Carlos Briceno in *Hispanic.* "I really felt I was being penalized for being the sex symbol they had created, and that made my Spanish blood boil." Despite the rumors, Welch continued to work in films. In 1974 she finally achieved critical recognition when she received a Golden Globe award for best actress for her part in *The Three Musketeers.*

In 1971 Welch had divorced Curtis. Six years later she met French screenwriter/producer Andre Weinfeld. After they were married in 1980, Weinfeld helped manage her career. Her 1981 television special, *From Raquel with Love,* which he helped produce, received high ratings. But that same year Welch was humiliated when she was replaced by Debra Winger after she had already begun work on the film *Cannery Row.* The company producing the movie claimed Welch had behaved unprofessionally on the set. She believed she had been fired to cut the costs of production. She sued the company for $20 million, but eventually lost the case.

Displays Wide Range of Talents

Welch was bitter over her firing and left Hollywood in 1981. Deciding she needed to take chances in her career, she accepted a role in a stage musical, *Woman of the Year.* Her singing and dancing performance was lauded by critics, and her reputation was beginning to transform. Her next role, as a tough Native American woman in the 1982 television movie *The Legend of Walks Far Woman,* showed she was capable of serious acting.

In 1984 Welch wrote a book, *The Raquel Welch Total Beauty and Fitness Program.* The book focused on preserving physical and mental health through yoga, diet, and exercise. Its success led the actress to release several home exercise videos that sold well.

During the late 1980s Welch took on a number of non-glamorous roles in television movies. In the 1987 film *Right to Die,* she portrayed a woman dying of amyotrophic lateral sclerosis, better known as Lou Gehrig's Disease. Critics praised her emotionally demanding performance, and many began to treat her as a serious actress. Welch was pleased. "I've always thought the older I get the more people would see that I have more to me than just my good looks," she explained to Briceno.

Despite success in many diverse roles, Welch's sexy image won't disappear. She accepts this, and continues to act and to promote exercise in the 1990s. For her many achievements, the Los Angeles Hispanic Women's Council named Welch its Woman of the Year in 1990.

For Further Information

Cosmopolitan, May 1990, pp. 320-24.
Haining, Peter, *Raquel Welch: Sex Symbol to Super Star,* St. Martin's Press, 1984.
Hispanic, April 1988, pp. 20-24.
Interview, September 1993, pp. 130+.

Emiliano Zapata

Mexican revolutionary
Born August 8, 1883, Anenecuilco, Morelos,
  Mexico
Died April 10, 1919, Morelos, Mexico

*"Seek justice from tyrannical governments
not with your hat in your hands but with a
rifle in your fist."*

Emiliano Zapata was a leader of the *campesinos* ("peasants") during the Mexican Revolution in the early 1900s. The Mexican dictator Porfirio Diaz, who gained control of the government in 1876, supported rich landowners who had seized the farming lands of the *campesinos* over the years. Without any say in the government, the powerless peasants sank deeper into poverty. When they finally rose in revolt, Zapata led the fight for the return of their stolen land. His many followers proudly called themselves Zapatistas. Although he died before the fighting ended, his memory lingers and is honored in stories, legends, and songs.

Zapata was born in the village of Anenecuilco in the Mexican state of Morelos. His family owned a small piece of land and some livestock. Even though a little better off economically than most *campesinos*, Zapata's family suffered many of the same problems. Portions of their land were unexpectedly taken over by the owners of neighboring haciendas, or huge plantations.

Zapata attended elementary school for only a short time and spent much of his youth learning to be a mule and horse trainer. After he was orphaned at 16, Zapata supported himself and his sisters in Anenecuilco by trading horses and working on the haciendas. Throughout Diaz's reign, called the *Porfiriato,* rich landowners continued to enlarge their haciendas by taking the lands of the *campesinos.* Any peasants who protested were jailed or killed.

By 1910, 30 hacienda owners controlled more than half the land in Morelos. Angered by their worsening situation, the peasants began to act. Because Zapata did not bow down to the rich landowners, the villagers of Anenecuilco trusted him and elected him president of the village council. His job was to safeguard the papers that showed the peasants' rightful ownership of the land that had been unjustly taken.

The Revolution Begins

In November 1910, Francisco Madero, the son of a wealthy rancher from northern Mexico, led the call for a rebellion to overthrow the Diaz government. At first, Zapata did not join the revolt. When Madero promised land reforms if he were elected to office, Zapata quickly gathered his men for the fight and the revolution was on. Zapata proved to be a skillful fighter and leader. He often outwitted the government soldiers and became a hero to the Zapatistas. By May 1911, rebel victories across Mexico forced Diaz to resign the presidency and to flee to Europe. In the new elections in October of that year, Madero won the presidency.

Madero did not live up to his promises. He had no plans to break up the haciendas and return land to the *campesinos.* Instead, he demanded the Zapatistas lay down their arms. Zapata and his men refused to do so

Emiliano Zapata

men began a new revolt. Since the Zapatistas had little food, clothing, and weapons, they fought by ambushing enemy villages and haciendas. After they looted what they needed, they gave the lands and anything else that remained to the *campesinos*.

In February 1913, Madero was suddenly murdered by his top general, Victoriano Huerta. Forces loyal to Madero quickly turned on Huerta and forced him from office in August 1914. A politician named Venustiano Carranza then took over the presidency.

While the government was rapidly changing hands, Zapata continued to press for land reforms. He submitted his plan to Carranza, but the new president rejected it and war seemed likely. Zapata then met with Pancho Villa, a bandit turned revolutionary. Villa controlled a large army in the northern part of Mexico. Carranza tried to keep the two revolutionaries from meeting, but he was unsuccessful. On December 4, 1914, Zapata and Villa met in the village of Xochimilco just outside of Mexico City. Together they planned to carry on the revolution against Carranza and his government.

The alliance between Zapata and Villa proved to be worthless. Villa and his Army of the North had promised to send weapons and other materials to the Zapatistas, but they never did. Lacking the needed supplies, Zapata and his men could not in turn support Villa. The Army of the North suffered crushing defeats, and government troops soon turned their attacks against the Zapatistas.

By the end of 1916, fighting was fierce all over the country, but the state of Morelos seemed to suffer the most. The state capital of Cuernavaca and hundreds of villages were destroyed, the sugar industry was ruined, and

until their demands for land reform were met. When they continued their revolt, Madero called them bandits.

In response, Zapata issued his own revolutionary platform in November 1911. Named the *Plan de Ayala*, it called for all illegally seized land to be returned to its rightful owners. The plan also demanded that the government take one-third of the land from each hacienda and give it to the *campesinos*. To prove he was not a bandit, Zapata organized committees to help distribute fairly any returned land. He also set up a bank to give loans to the *campesinos* who obtained land.

Zapata Fights for Land Reform

When the Madero government refused to listen to Zapata's demands, Zapata and his

Zapata, center, with his men c. 1914-1916 during U.S. expedition to Mexico

nearly half the people were killed. Those villagers not murdered were forced to settle in other regions of the country. The Zapatistas lost many men—they shrank from 20,000 to only 5,000. Even so, they remained a threat, attacking areas around Mexico City. Their methods were often as brutal as those of the government troops. At one point, the Zapatistas blew up a train, killing many civilians aboard.

Zapata regained control of Morelos in 1917, but the Zapatistas were falling apart. They were hungry and tired of fighting. Many wanted to sign a peace treaty with the government even if the *Plan de Ayala* were not accepted. Zapata, however, refused to give in. He vowed to fight until the government guaranteed land reform for the *campesinos*. Even though the peasants continued to back Zapata, many northern rebels did not. Without national support for their cause, the Zapatistas were doomed.

Zapata finally met his end in 1919. Jesus Guajardo, a colonel in the government army, tricked Zapata into believing he wanted to join the Zapatistas. At first, Zapata was suspicious of Guajardo's offer, but he finally agreed to meet Guajardo at the Hacienda de Chinameca. It was a trap. When Zapata and a few of his men rode into the walled estate, government soldiers were waiting. A bugle sounded and the soldiers fired. Zapata fell dead from his horse.

Guajardo delivered Zapata's body to the Municipal Palace to prove his death and to discourage the peasants. The Zapatistas were not convinced. Many believed Zapata was still alive, and claimed he had escaped on his beautiful white horse, *As de Oro.* Some even stated they saw him riding in the dead of night. Although the Zapatistas continued the fight, Zapata's original goals for land reform were never fully met. A peace settlement that did not include his *Plan de Ayala* was eventually reached between the Zapatistas and the government. Despite this setback, many people in Mexico have not forgotten Zapata's dedication to the fight for their rights. For them, he has remained a hero.

For Further Information

Parkinson, Roger, *Zapata: A Biography,* Stein and Day, 1980.

Ruiz, Ramon Eduardo, *The Great Rebellion: Mexico, 1905-1924,* Norton, 1980.

Travel Holiday, October 1990, pp. 46-54+.

Womack, John, *Zapata and the Mexican Revolution,* Knopf, 1968.

FIELD OF ENDEAVOR INDEX

30530000007678